QUESTIONS JESUS ASKED

BOOKS BY THE SAME AUTHOR

QUESTIONS
JESUS ASKED

CLOVIS G. CHAPPELL

ABINGDON-COKESBURY PRESS
New York • *Nashville*

QUESTIONS JESUS ASKED

SET UP, PRINTED, AND BOUND BY THE PARTHENON PRESS, AT NASHVILLE, TENNESSEE, UNITED STATES OF AMERICA

To Polly

*latest and littlest
of our dear grandbabies*

INTRODUCTION

IT has been said that the gospel is like a stone thrown into a pond of still water. At first the ripple created by the stone is small, but presently it becomes larger and larger until eventually it reaches the very banks of the pond.

Years ago a young man preached the pure gospel from his pulpit in America. At first he reached a comparatively small circle, but from the very start it was a circle of blessing, and the pool itself was not stagnant but of pure clear water which brought refreshment. Then later he moved to a bigger church and the circle widened and deepened. Presently he wrote down his thoughts, and a far wider circle was reached by his books. Some of them reached Britain in her day of fiery trial from aerial bombardment by a cruel and relentless enemy.

The people of Britain were forced to live in holes in the ground; some passed into "the land of far distances." In those days of terror the hearts of men and women in Britain were open. In underground tube stations the clergy conducted short services. There was one writer whom they had never seen, but whose words were heard, and that man was Clovis G. Chappell. From the United States of America he spoke sometimes through the mouths of others who read his sermons aloud.

It is with real pleasure that I bear testimony to the blessing and comfort of a friend whom, yet having not seen, I can say reverently I love. Each new book is better than the last. In confidence that he has kept the best wine until the last, I commend his latest work.

Some of our American cousins have sent us in Britain parcels of food. These have been most warmly appreciated, but Clovis Chappell has sent us the very bread of life received from his Master. We want to thank God and him for very great blessings received.

R. D. DAUNTON-FEAR

The Rectory
Gravesend, England

CONTENTS

9

I

THE FOLKS WHO ARE DIFFERENT

"What do ye more than others?"

MATTHEW 5:47

෧~෨

THIS is an arresting and searching question. It is evident that Jesus expects his followers to be vastly different from those about them. He came at a cost to himself beyond our powers to understand, to do something for us that we cannot do for ourselves. It was for the joy that was set before him, a joy measured in terms of transformed lives, that he endured the cross, despising the shame. Just what difference then has his coming made in your life and mine? What is there about us as professing Christians that is special? If there is nothing, then our Christianity is a futile something, a disappointment to ourselves, and a far keener disappointment to him whom we claim as our Lord and Master.

Naturally this difference between the man who is a Christian and the one who is not is not so sharp in our own land today as it was when Christianity was young. This difference is not so pronounced among us as it is in

11

pagan lands where the gospel has been only recently proclaimed. Our society has been so leavened by Christian teaching and preaching that there are multitudes who are Christian in certain of their attitudes, though they acknowledge no loyalty to Jesus Christ. Yet there is something really distinctive about those who know Jesus Christ. A little girl in India, when questioned about the Christians in her village, described them as "the folks who are different." That description holds good in every land and in every age.

As there is a marked difference between the man who follows Christ and the man who does not, there is also a marked kinship between one Christian and another. It is a matter of deep regret that we are divided into so many different sects and denominations. But in spite of this, as others have pointed out, real Christians are more alike than any other people in the world. Henry P. Van Dusen calls our attention to this in his book *They Found the Church There*. In telling how the Christians of the South Sea Islands took care of our soldier boys, he declares that this tender care was the same whether those showing it were Methodist, Catholic, Episcopalian, or any other denomination. As those who know Christ differ from those who do not, even so, real Christians are more alike than any other group in the world.

Assuming then that our Christianity is genuine, what is there distinctive about us? Perhaps we can get a clearer answer to this question by looking at the early church. Often we can see what is far off better than we can see what is near. As we turn the pages of the New Testament,

12

what do we find that the Christian possessed that his unbelieving neighbor did not possess? Of course our answer to this question can be only in part.

I

These early Christians specialized in what, for lack of a better word, I call brotherliness. As T. R. Glover would say, the Christian of the first century outloved his pagan neighbor. He was far more brotherly. There was a breadth and depth about his love that was beautifully distinctive.

1. These early Christians specialized in love one for another. They had been so taught by their Master. How, according to Jesus, are we to distinguish one who is a Christian from one who is not? "By this shall all men know that ye are my disciples, if. . . ." If what? Not if you belong to a certain denomination, not if you hold to certain beliefs or forms of worship. This is the one mark of genuineness: "If ye have love one to another."

It was by one Christian thus loving his fellow Christian that these early saints made perhaps their most profound impression upon the world of their day. "How these Christians love each other!" men exclaimed in awed wonder. And because these pagans longed to love and be loved, they were drawn into these Christian groups that Paul called colonies of heaven. To this day there is nothing so winsome as an atmosphere made warm and vital by the presence of those who really love each other. Such an atmosphere belongs to every truly Christian group. This is the case because every Christian loves his fellow Christian.

2. Not only did these followers of Jesus love one another, not only did they love the brotherhood, but they loved those outside the brotherhood. If you read *Out of the Night,* a best seller a few years ago, you must have been impressed by the author's emphasis on the devotion of one Communist to another. I could not help being amazed at the price that one fellow traveler seemed willing to pay to serve and protect another. But as impressive as was their loyalty to each other, so was their hatred of all outside their organization. There was no sacrifice too great for them to make in seeking to destroy all who happened not to be of their faith.

But not only did these early Christians love each other, they also loved strangers, foreigners, and outsiders. If our world is divided today by deep and wide chasms, that ancient world was divided by chasms that were deeper and wider still. Yet there was no chasm that separated people in that day that Christianity did not bridge. It bridged the chasm between man and man and between race and race. It bridged the chasm between people who were respectable and those who were outcast. It gave to social nobodies and slaves healing for their wounded self-respect by bringing them into the brotherhood. These early Christians were possessed of an eager interest in every human soul. They not only loved one another, but they loved strangers and outsiders.

3. Finally, these disciples of Jesus not only loved one another, not only did they love strangers and foreigners, but they loved their enemies. That is something that the man of the world not only does not do, but does not even

14

desire to do. In *Quo Vadis* Petronius is writing a letter to his nephew who has been converted to Christianity. This nephew has been impressing upon his uncle the fact that if he becomes a Christian he must love everybody, even his enemies. "Must I love Nero?" writes the uncle in reply. Then he answers his own question: "I swear by the white knees of the Graces that I couldn't love him if I wanted to." What is implied is that such love is not only impossible but undesirable.

But these Christians did love their enemies. Real Christians do so still. If they do not they are simply not Christians. Of course Christian love does not mean fondness for or delight in one's enemies. They are not the ones that we would choose as our guests. We love our enemies when we exercise toward them an active and sacrificial good will. Such love Jesus taught, such love Jesus practiced. "Bless them that curse you, . . . pray for them which despitefully use you, and persecute you," is his exacting word. So he himself did. He did it even as he hung on the cross. Here he threw about the shoulders of his murderers the sheltering folds of this protecting prayer: "Father, forgive them; for they know not what they do."

Here is another scene. A brilliant and gifted young man, Stephen by name, has become a follower of the Christ. He proclaims his faith with irresistible power. His foes, being unable to answer him with words, resort to stones. They drag him outside the city and mob him. There is no effort at justice or fair play. He is done to death without even a mock trial. How does he meet this terrible ordeal? He meets it in the spirit of his Master.

15

When we hear him pray this prayer, "Lord, lay not this sin to their charge," we know that we are in the presence of a Christian. These early Christians specialized in brotherliness in that they loved one another, they loved outsiders, they loved even their enemies. Such love is characteristic of Christ's real followers today.

II

Then these early Christians specialized in a fine gallantry that made them dare to live life the hard way. They went out, not simply to follow Christ, but to reproduce him. Thus they sought to make him king over all that pagan world. Their adventure was costly. Their Master had made this fact plain to them from the beginning. They had become followers of Jesus knowing that such would be the case. They knew that they would have to pay much, even their very all.

Jesus also makes this plain to us. He declares that there is a wide gate and an easy way, but that this leads to death. If we are bent on life we must enter by the narrow gate and travel the hard way. It was so hard for Jesus himself that it involved the cross. He never promised that it would be easier for us. He said: "If any man will come after me, let him deny himself, and take up his cross, and follow me." At the very door of entrance to life there stands a cross upon which we must die to self. This dying to self is often as painful as physical death. But there is no beginning of the Christian life without this dying to self. There is no continuing it without this

16

daily dying to ourselves. There simply is no cheap and easy way to be a Christian.

If you will turn the pages of your Bible with this in mind, you will be impressed by how little God seems to care for the ease and comfort of his saints. Take those men of the Old Testament who were most loyal to him and who became his closest friends. These heroic souls were willing to dare any danger, brave any death rather than prove disloyal. What response did God make to them? Did he see to it that no rude wind blew upon them? Did he shelter and coddle them? Here is the answer: "They were stoned, they were sawn asunder, were tempted, were slain with the sword: they wandered about in sheepskins and goatskins; being destitute, afflicted, tormented. . . . They wandered in deserts, and in mountains, and in dens and caves of the earth."

In the New Testament there is the same seeming indifference. For instance, when Jesus kneels in prayer for the last time with his little handful of friends he makes no plea that they be sheltered and protected. He knows the harsh and cruel world in which he is leaving them. They are destined, almost to a man, to die for their loyalty to him. Yet this is his prayer: "I pray not that thou shouldest take them out of the world, but that thou shouldest keep them from the evil." He is concerned not for their comfort, but for their character.

What is perhaps stranger still, this indifference on the part of God to the comfort and ease of his saints was shared by these saints themselves. Notice in the New Testament how the followers of Jesus prayed when they

17

found themselves with their backs to the wall. Their prayers were never for escape. Those who prayed only to escape were not followers of Christ. Here are the two revolutionaries who died at the side of Jesus. One of them is a truly great soul. After he has taken the part of Jesus against those who are doing him to death, he prays this prayer for himself: "Lord, remember me when thou comest into thy kingdom." He wants deliverance, not from where he is, even though he is suffering the pangs of hell. He rather seeks deliverance from what he is. But the lesser revolutionary does not mind being what he is; he only hates being where he is. Therefore he prays this prayer: "If thou be Christ, save thyself and us."

Simon Magus has sought to buy the Holy Spirit on a cash basis. With righteous indignation Peter turns on him with this word: "Thy money perish with thee. . . . Repent therefore of this thy wickedness, and pray God, if perhaps the thought of thine heart may be forgiven thee. For I perceive that thou art in the gall of bitterness, and in the bond of iniquity." Then answered Simon and said: "Pray ye to the Lord for me." But what are Peter and John to ask for him? Not that he be forgiven, but "that none of these things which ye have spoken come upon me." He had no desire for any kind of heaven; he only wanted to escape hell.

But listen to the saints as they pray: "And now, Lord, behold their threatenings." Who are doing the threatening? The very same men who had crucified their Master. They know, therefore, that these are not vain threats. Their danger is real. For what then do they pray? They

18

do not ask for escape. This is their prayer: "Grant unto thy servants, that with all boldness they may speak thy word." They do not ask for an easy way. They ask rather that they may see their hard way through with honor.

Here is Paul writing a letter from a prison in Rome. By and by he comes to the matter of prayer. "Praying always with all prayer and supplication in the Spirit, and watching thereunto with all perseverance and supplication for all saints," he urges. Then he remembers his own needs. Therefore he requests prayer for himself. But for what are his friends to ask on his behalf? That he might be free? That his health might no longer be endangered by his hard prison life? By no means. "And for me," he writes, "that utterance may be given unto me, that I may open my mouth boldly, to make known the mystery of the gospel, for which I am an ambassador in bonds." Thus in a fashion characteristic of the saints, he does not ask for an easy way; he rather seeks for strength and courage to walk the hard way. These early Christians dared to walk the difficult road. The same must be true of us.

III

But here is a lovely paradox. If these early Christians did have the hardest time of anybody, they also had the best time of anybody. When we get our first glimpse of them as a group they are so absurdly joyous that the worldlings as they look on can find no explanation of their joy but that they have had a few too many drinks. "These men," they declare, "are full of new wine." But from that intoxication they never recovered. It did not leave them with an ill head and an aching heart. It rather sent them laughing and singing over all that hard Roman world.

Real Christians are joyful. We cannot be like our Master in any other way. I know that we have a tendency to gasp with amazement when we hear Jesus say "My yoke is easy." What was his yoke? It was the yoke of a perfectly dedicated life. It was a yoke that made his life one long toil up Calvary. Yet he tells us that the yoke that cost him so much was kindly. This was certainly true. In spite of the cross, yes, and because of the cross, Jesus lived more richly, more joyously, I take it, than any other man who ever set foot upon this planet.

The abundant life that Jesus lived he shares with his followers. Take another look at Paul, for example. What a hard life he lived! He went to the whipping post so many times that his body must have been little more than one huge scar. He tells us frankly that he suffered the loss of all things. Yet how richly he lived! Absolutely nothing could rob him of his radiance. But this radiance belongs not simply to the Christian of the first century, but of every century. This is the case because specializing in loving and in self-giving, he specializes also in the fellowship of his Lord. The Christian thus possessing Christ possesses all that makes life supremely worth while, both in time and in eternity.

II

THE ANTIDOTE FOR WORRY

"Which of you by taking thought can add one cubit unto his stature?"

MATTHEW 6:27

$\backsim$

WHAT warning is Jesus giving us by this arresting question? To begin negatively, he is not warning us against taking life seriously. Jesus was tremendously in earnest. No man was ever more so. One day as his disciples looked into his face they read there the interpretation of a text that they had not understood before. That was this: "The zeal of thine house hath eaten me up." That is, Jesus was fairly burning himself out because of his intense earnestness. He desires us to be in earnest. Therefore he is not urging upon us that happy-go-lucky attitude toward life that some pretend. There are those the soil of whose souls is so shallow that it cannot even grow a decent worry.

No more is Jesus warning us against the thought-out life. Few words of Jesus, in my opinion, have been more grossly misunderstood than what he had to say about

21

taking thought. When, for instance, he said, "Take therefore no thought for the morrow," he was not forbidding us to look ahead. If ever a man took thought for tomorrow, Jesus was that man. It was he "who for the joy that was set before him endured the cross, despising the shame." Since he thought of tomorrow he would have us do the same. Therefore he is not warning here against the thought-out life.

What then is he warning against? He is warning against our taking anxious thought for tomorrow. He is eager that we face the future with an attitude of faith instead of an attitude of feverish and fretful anxiety. Thus he appeals to our common sense with his question: "Which of you by taking thought [or being anxious] can add one cubit unto his stature?"

I

Why do we need a word like this?

1. We need it because so many of us are worried. Perhaps there was never another day in all history when there were so many worried people as there are at this moment. Nor can we explain this widespread worry merely in terms of our circumstances. Many of our circumstances are bad enough, it is true. But worry is not a child of circumstances. Whether you worry or not depends not upon your situation but upon you. Whenever you are robbed by worry it is always an inside job.

But be the causes what they may, multitudes are worried today. Ignorant folks worry. Of course they do not know any better. Educated folks worry. Certainly. They know so much to worry about. Old folks worry. Yes, indeed. They are coming close to the sunset of the evening star. Young folks worry. Naturally. They have so many years ahead of them in our topsy-turvy world. Irreligious folks worry because they have no faith. Many religious folk worry because they have an inadequate faith. All sorts of people worry.

Not only do all sorts of people worry, but they worry about all sorts of things. We worry about our bodies and we worry about our souls. We worry about the pulpit and the pulpit worries about the pew. We worry about getting married and we worry because we have got married. We worry about calamities that actually take place. We worry far more about calamities that never take place. If you are a good worrier and put in more than a forty-hour week, as many of us do, you can count on it that at least 75 to 90 per cent of the tragedies about which you have worried never have and never will take place.

Not only do all sorts of folks worry about all sorts of things, but, as another has pointed out, they worry at the worst possible times. If you would only do all your worrying while on vacation, then it might not be so bad. But instead of picking a good leisurely time, you wait until the going is hard and until the burden is heavy. You wait until you are most in need of steady nerves and a clear head. Then you unfit yourself for coping with your situation by giving way to worry.

2. Then we need this word of warning because worry is so useless. This is the very heart of what Jesus is implying. "Which of you by being anxious can add one

23

cubit unto his stature?" If it so happens that you are not as tall as you desire to be, you will not grow taller by merely worrying about it. We have all done plenty of useless things, but nobody ever did anything more useless than to worry. It never gets us anywhere. It never lifted a single load. It never solved a single problem. It never rubbed out a single wrinkle. But it has rubbed in billions of them.

It has been well said that there are two classes of things about which nobody ought to worry. First, we ought not to worry about those things that we cannot help. There are some things that, if we are wise, we simply accept. We may object to the law of gravity, but it is not wise to argue with that law. This is the case because it will not argue with us; it will only break our bones. There are many things that we might like to avoid if we could, but we simply cannot. Therefore we ought to meet them without anxiety.

Take the matter of growing old, for instance. I have known those who lived in deadly fear of the almanac. There are perhaps some of you who would not tell your ages for any price. There is no gain in that. Folks are guessing at you. By telling your age you might save yourself a year or two. Why should we fear to get old? Does not God have as much plan for December as for June? Yet a friend said to me the other day: "You ought not to get old." I replied: "The only way I know how to avoid it is to die and that is too heroic a remedy for me to be willing to apply it at this time."

A second class of things that nobody ought to worry

about are those things that we can help. Instead of worrying about them, we ought to get so busy helping that we shall not have time to worry. But did you ever wake up on a winter's night about two thirds cold and remember that there was a blanket not six feet away? But instead of getting up and getting the blanket you simply lay there and worried the rest of the night. Of course such conduct did not get you warm, but you had a good time worrying. We ought to avoid anxiety because it is so useless.

3. We need this warning because worry is so harmful. It is harmful to the one who worries. It takes a great deal of work to kill if there is peace within the heart of the worker. But it does not take worry long to make us face toward the cemetery. This ugly sin is the mother of many a disease, and there is no disease known to medicine that it does not aggravate.

Not only does worry hurt the one who worries, but it makes such a one hard to live with. I have known husbands who would be cheerful all day long at their work, then come home at eventide and spill out all their worries about the dinner table and spoil everybody's appetite except their own. I have known a few wives who were so worried that the best they could offer their husbands and children when they came home from the day's work was a face that looked like a dead ache. Those who worry are a burden to themselves, a burden to others, and above all else, they are a disappointment to our Lord. When Jesus was here how often he had to say to his friends with pained amazement: "O men, how little you trust me!"

25

II

Since worry is such an ugly foe we ought not to tolerate it. It is more than a misfortune; it is a positive sin. Therefore we must get rid of it. But how?

There are two so-called remedies that are very popular, but they can be guaranteed not to work. For instance, some of us who are worried now are going to quit worrying just as soon as we get into an ideal situation. But that remedy is an utter failure. This is the case for at least three good reasons. It is a failure in the first place because there is no ideal situation. It is a failure in the second place because if there were an ideal situation, the chances are that you and I would not get into it. It is a failure in the third place because even if there were an ideal situation and you and I were so fortunate as to get into it, the first thing we would do would be to mess it up.

If we cannot conquer worry by getting into an ideal situation, no more can we conquer it by merely clenching our fists and squaring our jaws and saying: "Go to, now, I am never going to worry again as long as I live." I used to have a friend who, when she began to become feverish with anxiety, would say over and over again: "I am not going to worry about that, would you?" But the more she resolved the more desperately worried she became. I have an idea that she got to heaven several years ahead of time because she found no better remedy against worry than grim determination.

What then are we to do?

1. First, I think it might help if we bear in mind that

26

worry is an acquirement. Nobody was ever born worried. You doubtless caused somebody else to worry soon after you got here, but nobody was ever born worried. If it so happens that you are an excellent violinist or a skilled golfer, it is not because you were born that way; it is rather because you have practiced and practiced and practiced. Even so, if it happens that you are good at worrying, that is the case because you have practiced and practiced and practiced. Worry is an achievement. Anything that we can learn can be unlearned.

2. If we are to conquer worry we must keep on good terms with our consciences. We are gifted with a conscience, every one of us. If we are to have peace we must give ear to that inner voice. H. G. Wells says of a certain character that he was not so much a personality as a civil war. Such civil wars we have all met. These have little chance of making a winning fight against an outside enemy; they are too busy fighting themselves.

Is there a certain course of action that others seem able to follow with impunity but that always leaves you with a feeling of being defeated and morally run down at the heel? If such is the case, however innocent such conduct may seem, you will never know peace until you give it up. Does God seem to be pointing down a certain road saying to you, "Walk that way"? Then you will never find peace until you obey. When Isaiah said, "There is no peace . . . unto the wicked," he was uttering a truth that is as up-to-date as your latest heartbeat! We can never find peace until we stop fighting with God and our own consciences.

3. If we are to find peace some of us will have to re-

direct our thinking. We will have to look sometimes upon the things that we approve and not sorely upon those of which we disapprove. Paul put it in these words: "Whatsoever things are true, whatsoever things are honest, whatsoever things are just, whatsoever things are pure, whatsoever things are lovely, whatsoever things are of good report; if there be any virtue, and if there be any praise, think on these things."

The apostle is not urging us to a blind optimism. He is not trying to make us into starry-eyed Pollyannas. He is not even telling us to look on the bright side. He is rather urging upon us the sanity of seeking in our world, in our situation, in our church, in our friends, in our loved ones, the things that are lovely instead of fixing our whole attention upon those things that are ugly and that fill us with horror and disgust. If we are going to conquer worry we must give attention to the beautiful as well as to the ugly. We must seek to think white instead of allowing ourselves constantly to think black.

4. Finally, the supreme antidote against worry is faith in God. The same fatherly God, Jesus reminds us, who looks after the needs of the birds can be trusted to supply our needs. We are to rest in the Lord and wait patiently for him. We are to cast all our care upon him in the realization that he cares for us. Above all else, we are to make a habit of prayer. Paul, who shared the mind of Christ to an unusual degree, gives us this wise word: "In every thing by prayer and supplication with thanksgiving let your requests be made known unto God. And the peace of God,

which passeth all understanding, shall keep your hearts and minds through Christ Jesus."

I read somewhere of an aviator who was making a flight around the world. After he had been gone for some two hours from his last landing field, he heard a noise in his plane which he recognized as the gnawing of a rat. He realized that while his ship was grounded the rat had entered it and was now getting in his work. Not knowing what bit of his delicate machine those sharp teeth might be cutting, he was filled with fear. At first he did not know what to do. It was two hours back to the landing field and more than two hours to the next one ahead.

Then he remembered that the rat is a rodent. It is not made for the heights; it is made to live on the ground and under the ground. Therefore the pilot began to climb. He went up a thousand feet, then another thousand, and still another thousand, until he was twenty thousand feet in the air. Then the gnawing ceased. When more than two hours later he came down in safety at the next landing field, there was a dead rat in the pit of the plane.

Worry is a rodent. It cannot live "in the secret place of the most High." It cannot breathe in an atmosphere made vital by prayer. Therefore "in every thing by prayer and supplication with thanksgiving let your requests be made known unto God."

> "Drop thy still dews of quietness,
>   Till all our strivings cease;
>   Take from our souls the strain and stress,
>   And let our ordered lives confess
>   The beauty of thy peace."

29

III

THE HABIT OF FAULTFINDING

"Why beholdest thou the mote that is in thy brothers' eye, but considerest not the beam that is in thine own eye?"

MATTHEW 7:3

൧

THERE is a delicious touch of humor about this text. Jesus is deadly serious, but that fact does not interfere with his laughter. There are those who confuse seriousness with solemnity. Such people are convinced that to be serious one must be very solemn. Now, while it is possible for one to be very serious and have his eyes bright with tears, it is possible for another to be very serious and have his eyes bright with laughter. Jesus had a sense of humor. He knew that laughter is a good medicine. He knew also that it is a very effective weapon. What could be more absurd than for a man with a log in his eye to minister to another who is afflicted with a mote, a mere speck? Thus did Jesus seek to make the sin of faultfinding look ridiculous, and to laugh it out of court.

It is well to bear in mind that in rebuking the seeker

after specks Jesus is not forbidding us to reach a conclusion as to the degree of worthfulness of those with whom we have to do. Such conclusions are at once inevitable and necessary. This is indicated by the Master's next word: "Give not that which is holy unto the dogs, neither cast ye your pearls before swine." It is impossible to carry out this command unless we reach some conclusion as to who is swinish and who is not. What Jesus is really rebuking is faultfinding—the looking for the worst instead of the best.

I

Why do you see the mote in your brother's eye? It is not because it is so large and glaring that it cannot be overlooked. It is not because it shrieks at you and demands attention. When you see a thing so small that it can float in a sunbeam it is because you are looking for it. You cannot help seeing a log. It compels your attention. But no one is likely to see a mote, an insignificant speck, unless he is a keen-eyed searcher.

And why do we search for specks? Generally speaking, we do so because we hope to find something wrong. We feel that we cannot afford to give the individual thus criticized a clean bill of health. Satan, in the immortal drama of Job, is of this type. When the Lord calls attention to the high character of his servant Job, Satan fairly shakes with laughter. He cannot help being amazed at how easily the Lord is taken in. "Doth Job fear God for nought?" he questions. What he is suggesting is that Job is not really a good man. In fact, there is no such thing as goodness. Decent in his outward conduct he may be, but

31

he is rotten in motive. Thus Satan was so keen-eyed that he could see a speck that was at once invisible and non-existent—a bad motive. Even so, when we see motes it is because we are looking for them and hope to find them.

Why do we hope to find something wrong? We do so for a variety of reasons. Sometimes we look for the worst in order to salve our own consciences. When our own faults and follies and failures make us uncomfortable we often seek to gather a bit of comfort by saying, "I am not the only one." Such people feel that the number of the guilty in some way lessens the guilt of the individual. But of course that is not the case. If I am dying of a disease it will not help me in the least to know that thousands of others are dying of the same deadly disease. Yet we sometimes seek comfort in our moral sickness by looking at the faults of others and convincing ourselves that theirs are as great or greater than our own.

Then we often indulge in faultfinding because we have a strong conviction that by tearing the other fellow down we somehow build ourselves up. For instance, when I tell what a shabby and shoddy minister a certain pastor is, I do this in order that you may, by comparison, realize what a paragon of perfection I am. "Poor Mary," said an over-fed sister the other day. "Poor Mary, she really ought to reduce." Why this criticism? It was the critic's way of adding to her own slenderness without going to the trouble of changing her menu. But we really never build ourselves up by tearing others down. I have never known any man to build a house by tearing down the house of his neighbor.

Finally, we often find fault out of sheer envy. Of all the vices, surely envy is one of the most malignant. It is not, as another has pointed out, to be confused with jealousy. Jealousy may be a perfectly natural and right emotion. I know that at times it is "the green-eyed monster which doth mock the meat it feeds on," but when the meat is made to order by another, then jealousy is all but inevitable. If a husband gives his love to another woman who is not his wife, that wife has a right to be jealous. Jealousy is a child of love.

But envy is a child of hate. "Love envieth not." Envy has a long and ugly criminal record. When Cain's offering was rejected and Abel's accepted, Cain could not take it. Out of envy he struck his brother dead. Saul flung a dart at David and then drove himself mad out of envy. The elder son out of envy did his best to spoil the feast when his prodigal brother had come home. It was envy that helped to crucify our Lord. Sometimes we inflict the pangs of crucifixion by our tongues because of envy. Thus we find fault to salve our own consciousness, to build ourselves up, and out of sheer envy.

II

Why is this practice of looking for motes so wrong?

1. It is wrong in motive. Of course there is such a thing as constructive criticism. We realize the truth of this word: "Faithful are the wounds of a friend." A real friend may point out the faults of one he is earnestly seeking to help. This text does not urge us to go about soft-soaping all and sundry. But the man who is seeking

33

the worst is not actuated by good will. This man with a log in his eye claimed to be trying to help his brother, but in so claiming he was playing the hypocrite. His motive was one of sheer selfishness.

In one of the beautiful scenes of the New Testament, Mary broke a cruse of oil and anointed her Lord. Jesus saw in it something so lovely that he declared that he would never allow it to be forgotten. The perfume of that gracious deed filled the room on that distant day. Not only so, but it has helped to sweeten our world for nineteen hundred years. But Judas, with a keen eye for the worst, saw in it nothing beautiful at all. He saw in it only something to snarl over. "Why was not this ointment sold for three hundred pence, and given to the poor?" he asked in indignation. It seems at first glance a very reasonable question. But what prompted Judas to offer this criticism? He did not offer it for the sake of Mary, nor for the sake of the poor, nor for the sake of the Master. He offered it out of sheer selfishness. The faultfinder is wrong in his motive.

2. This practice of looking for the worst instead of the best is bad because it so often hurts the one with whom we find fault. There are those who are deeply wounded by such criticism. There are those who are discouraged by it. Then often the faultfinder steals the reputation and thus impairs the usefulness of the one criticized. My reputation is a part of the capital on which I do business. If one robs me of it, doors of usefulness will thereby be shut in my face that might otherwise have remained open. The faultfinder often hurts the one with whom he finds fault.

34

3. Finally, the habit of looking for the worst instead of the best hurts the critic himself. The faultfinder may wound his brother, but he inflicts the sorest wound upon himself. Why is this the case?

First, it is the case because the habit of faultfinding has a way of putting out our eyes. The faultfinder is never a dependable factfinder. This is true because to seek the worst is to find the worst. It is true here as elsewhere that he that seeketh findeth. To find the worst and to fix our eyes upon it is to miss the best. In looking for something to condemn we fail to see anything to commend. Even Jesus Christ himself had no moral beauty for those who were seeking only to find fault. To seek for the worst is to become blind to the best. You cannot count on the faultfinder as a reliable factfinder.

Tell me what you are seeking and I will tell you what you are likely to find in your brother, in your situation, everywhere.

> "Pussy cat, pussy cat,
>   Where have you been?
> I've been to London
>   To visit the Queen.
>
> Pussy cat, pussy cat,
>   What did you there?
> I frightened a mousey
>   Right under her chair."

Here is one who has been on a visit to the metropolis. London, I think, is the most interesting city in the world. But when this cat had returned and her friends, who had never had an opportunity to visit London, gathered to hear of that famous city, they must have been sorely disappointed. This traveler had nothing to tell of London Tower with its heroic and bloody memories; nothing of Westminster Abbey, that poem in stone, with its sainted dead. She had nothing to say of the Houses of Parliament, nothing of Buckingham Palace, nothing even of the graciousness of the Queen. All she saw was a mouse. She saw only a mouse because, being mouse-minded, that was all she was looking for. She reported truly what she saw, but her report had no light to throw on the city. She had failed to see it.

If I were desirous of knowing the facts about a rugged land of poetry and beauty, I would not send a vulture to spy it out. In one respect he would be well-equipped for the task. But though he might fly over mountains crowned with forests, over many a lovely cottage nestling among the trees, and over waterfalls hanging like white ribbons from the cliffs, he would have nothing to say of any of these beauties. The one fact which he would report would be that he found a bit of carrion under a thornbush. Why would this be the case? It would not be so because that was all that was there. It would be the case because that would be all he was looking for.

One day you went to church in a critical frame of mind. You were in a mood to find fault. What was the result? Though the music was beautiful, the scripture lesson a gem, the sermon so full of truth that you agreed with it 99 per cent, yet you were not edified. This was because the minister said just one thing that offended you. There was one word in the sermon that you did not like. But instead of rejecting the little that was bad and accepting the much that was good, you threw away the good and kept only the objectionable. Had I desired an accurate account of that service I could not have obtained it from you. The faultfinder cannot be counted on for the truth. He is a bad factfinder.

Not only does the faultfinder miss the facts about his brother, but he misses those about himself as well. Generally speaking, the keener our eyes become to the faults of others, the blinder do they become to what is wrong with ourselves. The more we magnify the vices of our brother, the more do we minimize our own. It is equally true that the more we minimize his virtues, the more do we magnify our own. Thus we still hear one who is doing nothing to help heal the world's open sore saying pridefully, "At least I am not a hypocrite." What a noble boast! Neither is a tiger or a jackal or a fishing worm. No man is a saint because of one ugly sin of which he happens not to be guilty.

This blindness to his own faults is just what has overtaken this man who was looking for specks. What a joke it was when, with a whole log in his eye, he goes to his friend and dares to say: "Pardon me, but there is a speck in your eye. Let me help you." But our laughter is changed to tears when we realize that the poor fellow is not joking at all. He is in earnest. Thus that which might have been merely ludicrous becomes genuinely tragic. So long had this man looked for the faults of others that he had become totally blind to his own.

37

4. Then the faultfinder cheats himself in the realm of friendship. If you really desire to know how to win friends and influence people, I cannot give you all the rules that will work, but I can give you one that will not work. You will not win friends by constantly seeking for the worst in those about you and then telling them wherein they are wrong. If you have a friend you may lose him just by persistently picking him to pieces. If you have an enemy you may change him into a friend by looking for what is best in him and by telling him of your appreciation of that best. Here the word of Jesus is emphatically true: "With what measure ye mete, it shall be measured to you again."

5. Finally, the habit of faultfinding so ministers to our pride that it makes repentance next to impossible. Generally speaking, the faultfinder is an egotist. He is proud of his capacity to see more through a keyhole than others can see through a wide-open door. Iago, the worst devil in literature, was a man of this type. This is his proud boast: "I am nothing if not critical." Instead of being ashamed of his wickedness, he took pride in it. He was therefore as far from repentance as the Pharisee who went to the temple to pray, but got so busy cataloguing the vices of others that he forgot to ask for God's mercy and pardon for himself. The lesser robber who died by the side of Jesus might have repented had he not been so busy criticizing others. The greater robber went right where his companion went wrong. He took a look at himself. Therefore he declared that though he was suffering the very pangs of hell, he was suffering justly. It was thus

38

that repentance was born. No man ever finds God by confessing the sin of his brother. He has to confess and repent of his own.

Why then do we so often cheat ourselves by looking for petty faults? Such a habit is as silly as it is wicked. It is a sure way of ministering to our own wretchedness. However fine your friend, however lovely your home, however adorable your wife, however faithful your husband, just practice the habit of looking for the worst and all the glamour will fade away. However loyal your employer or employee, however excellent your position, constantly seek to find something to criticize adversely and soon you will be changing jobs. The habit of looking for specks may hurt others, but it will certainly inflict its deadly harm upon the faultfinder.

III

How then are we to find a cure for this ugly habit?

1. Let us realize the wickedness of it. Such a habit is not simply our peculiarity, it is our deadly sin. It is a cruel weapon by which we wound ourselves, our fellows, and our Lord. Such conduct can be natural only to an unregenerate and unbrotherly heart.

2. Having faced the wickedness of this habit, we are to repent. Repentance means a change of mind. It is so to change our minds that we not only cease our faultfinding, but we go in the opposite direction. Just as we once cultivated the habit of looking for something to condemn, we are now, by the grace of God, to cultivate the habit of looking for something to commend. Thus looking for the

best we are sure to find it, for it is true here also that he who seeketh findeth.

One day years ago my small son came running into my study to invite me to come and see a strange dog that had come to visit us. I hurried out only to find about the most disreputable-looking cur I had ever beheld. "What a horrible-looking creature," I exclaimed. But the boy saw him through different eyes. Therefore he was quick in his defense. "But, Daddy," he said, "he wags his tail good." Thus looking for the best, he found it. We can cultivate this habit and thus help others as well as oureslves.

"There are loyal hearts, there are spirits brave,
    There are souls that are pure and true;
Then give to the world the best you have,
    And the best will come back to you."

IV

THE HAND OF FAITH

*"O thou of little faith, wherefore didst thou
doubt?"*

MATTHEW 14:31

❧

JESUS put this question to Simon Peter after that
daring disciple had turned a triumph into a near
tragedy. You will notice that to the Master's question
Peter gave no answer. That is out of the ordinary. Doubt
is usually quite vocal. It can pour out niagaras of words
in defense of its position, and often look quite keen-eyed
and broad-browed while so doing. But on the pages of the
Bible, and especially in the presence of Jesus, it does not
show up so well. Often it looks quite unreasonable. Such
is surely the case in this fascinating story. If it is true
that the parables of Jesus are miracles of wisdom, it is also
true that his miracles are parables of teaching. They are
at once both timely and timeless. Therefore they have
something of value to say to us.

I

Look at Simon's fine beginning.

He with his fellow disciples is in a small vessel on the

41

Sea of Galilee. This little sea is being whipped into a rage by a tempest. Against the fierce opposition of the storm these fighting and frightened men are making little progress. Though it is now three o'clock in the morning they are but little nearer their goal than when they set out hours ago. More than once have they said to themselves and to each other that they wished that the Master would come. Then, as if in answer to their longing, they see him coming across the waves.

But his coming at first brings them no gladness. Our Lord often comes to us in a fashion that fills us more with fear than with comfort. Sometimes he comes in the guise of a keen disappointment or a heavy heartache. Sometimes he comes in a call to a high adventure of faith that we are not willing to make. I think it might amaze us to realize how many of us are really afraid of God—afraid, not in a beautiful and filial fashion, but rather in a fashion that makes us unwilling to surrender to him wholly lest he should demand too much of us.

Jesus, realizing that they were afraid, spoke to them this word of comfort: "Be of good cheer; it is I; be not afraid." "Be of good cheer." That word was upon the lips of Jesus again and again. He uttered it in the face of the ravages that sin had made; he uttered it as he reached the end of the journey and faced what seemed to be disastrous defeat. "In the world," he declared, "ye shall have tribulation: but be of good cheer; I have overcome the world." He implied: "I have overcome the fear of it and the love of it; I have overcome the worst it could do to me, and have changed that worst into the best."

42

Now, on hearing that word, "Be of good cheer," Simon's fear gave way to faith. He at once began to dream of doing the impossible. Jesus ever inspires faith. When one day his disciples came upon him at prayer they were deeply moved. Here was prayer that was so beautiful and real that it made their own prayer life seem paltry and cheap. They realized that they had never really prayed, at least not in this fashion. But if what they saw rebuked them, it also gave them hope. As they thus looked upon the Master they said, "We too can pray." Therefore they came eagerly and expectantly saying, "Lord, teach us to pray."

Not only does Jesus inspire faith by what he says and by what he does; he inspires faith through the faith of others. How much we owe to our fellow believers! There are those in whose presence it is easy to doubt. But there are also those in whose presence it is easy to believe the highest and the best. When my own lamp of faith has burned low I have gone again and again to relight it at the glowing torches of some of the choice believers whom I have known along the way.

Now as soon as Simon began to believe, he was ready for action. Faith is an active something. A Gallup poll revealed the fact that some 99 per cent of the American people claim to believe in God. But what is their faith doing for them? Is it helping them to conquer their lust for power, for money, for the unclean? What we really believe shapes our character and our conduct. When a certain crackedbrained adventurer decided centuries ago that the world was round instead of flat, he could not rest

43

until he had done something about it. It is impossible to take very seriously the professed faith of many of those composing this 99 per cent. Too many of them act as if the Bible were a myth and God a lie.

When Simon reached the conviction that with the presence of Jesus the impossible was possible he did something. He said: "Lord, if it be thou, bid me come unto thee on the water." How did the Master answer him? He did not rebuke him. Instead of telling Simon he was foolish, instead of warning him against being a starry-eyed fanatic, he rather invited him to adventure.

Just as Jesus inspires faith, he also encourages it. As we turn the pages of the New Testament we find that nothing thrilled him more than faith. Here is the story of a pagan who fairly swept Jesus off his feet by the fullness of his faith. He was a Roman centurion. When a slave of this officer became ill he so took the illness of that slave upon himself that he asked certain Jewish friends to appeal to Jesus on his behalf. This Roman soldier must have been a great soul. His brotherliness bridged the chasm between master and slave, Gentile and Jew, conqueror and conquered. In spite of the fact that he belonged to an army of occupation he had won the confidence and the friendship of the people he had been sent to rule. Therefore when these Jews appealed to Jesus they said he was worthy, "for he loveth our nation."

In answer to their prayers Jesus at once set out to visit this sick slave. But when this officer saw him coming he sent a messenger saying, in effect: "Never mind about coming. I am not worthy that you should enter my house, but speak the word only and my servant shall be healed. As a Roman soldier I have soldiers under me. When I give them orders they obey. You who have under you the healing might of God himself need only speak the word and my slave shall be healed." At that Jesus declared joyfully that he had not found so great faith even in Israel. Jesus always appreciated and encouraged faith.

When, therefore, Simon sought to do the impossible Jesus encouraged him. He did so with one word: "Come." When the Master said "Come," Simon at once began to climb out of the boat. That was faith. Had I been in Simon's place I should have desired far more than that one word of invitation. I should have wanted specific assurance on the part of Jesus that he would help me see it through. But Simon knew that the invitations of Jesus are guarantees that power will be given to the invited to accept. If this were not the case such invitations would not in reality be invitations at all, but mere mockery. Therefore believing that he can do what Jesus invites him to do, Simon boldly climbed out of the boat. Does it look silly? By no means when we face the facts. Upon what was Simon depending for safety while he remained in the boat? Upon a few planks. What was his confidence when he climbed out? His confidence was in the everlasting arms. He was depending upon the power of him in the hollow of whose hand the seas rage and roar.

Now thus depending upon the word of Christ, for a time at least he triumphed. No subsequent failure can do away with that fact. He did the impossible. So have countless thousands of others. There are those of us who

45

have thus won through difficulties that we could not have faced in our own strength. To the man who believes, always the impossible becomes possible. While Simon trusted he triumphed, and thus he was an inspiration to his friends and a joy to his Lord.

II

But when we look again something has gone wrong. Simon is sinking as if his Lord were out of the picture altogether. What is the matter? It is not that his Master's arm has grown weak or weary. It is not that the tempest has become too strong. The cause is rather this: Simon's faith has given way to fear. He has come to doubt. That is ever a supreme cause of failure. To doubt is always to sink.

"Without faith," says the writer to the Hebrews, "it is impossible to please him." We might leave off the latter part of the sentence and it would still be true. "Without faith it is impossible." What is impossible? Everything constructive is impossible. Without faith it is impossible to get married; it is impossible to build a home or to keep one; it is impossible to run a bank or any other business. Without faith it is impossible to win a permanent peace. It is faith that does all the constructive work that is done in the world.

Just as nothing of worth is possible through doubt, everything is possible through faith. So Jesus declared in language that sounds to us extravagant, even incredible. He said that a bit of faith that is genuine, even if no larger than a mustard seed, is mightier than an atomic bomb.

46

He was sure that such faith could toss mountains about. For instance, one day a father brought to him his afflicted son. Jesus was away at the time. Therefore his disciples tried to heal the boy, but failed. In the presence of their failure the father's faith began to slip. When Jesus came, the best that this father could pray was this: "If thou canst do any thing, have compassion on us, and help us."

At this Jesus looked at him with mingled amazement and pity. He was putting the "if" in the wrong place. "If thou canst believe, all things are possible to him that believeth." Then the father cried out with tears: "Lord, I believe; help thou mine unbelief." His was not a perfect faith, but it made the impossible to become possible. That is a unique and yet oft-repeated story. Jesus is saying today when we give him the opportunity what he often said in the long ago: "Go thy way: thy faith hath made thee whole." But without faith we constantly thwart his purpose for us. He can still do no mighty work for those who refuse to believe.

III

To faltering Simon, Jesus puts this question: "Wherefore didst thou doubt?" Why indeed? We do not all doubt for the same reason.

1. Some doubt is born of wishful thinking. I know that we who believe are accused of being the victims of wishful thinking. At times this may be true. But wishful thinking certainly works both ways. There are those who doubt in order to evade moral responsibility. The fool of whom the psalmist writes was such a man. "The fool hath said in

his heart, There is no God." He did not deny God in his head but in his heart. The fact of God put him at a high altitude where breathing was a bit difficult. It compelled him to face responsibilities that he did not desire to face. Therefore he dismissed God. Sometimes we doubt because we will to doubt.

2. There are those who doubt because of God's strange ordering of things. John the Baptist is a good example of this kind of doubter. He was a great and loyal soul. He had staked everything on his faith in Jesus Christ. For his loyalty he is now languishing in prison instead of carrying on his work in the big outside world. Rumors are being blown to him in his gloomy prison of how the Young Prophet is working wonders in the outer world. He is cleansing lepers and opening blind eyes. If he can do these impossible tasks for others, why does he not open the prison cell of one who has been a loyal friend? To this question John finds no satisfactory answer. Therefore, filled with doubt, he appeals to Jesus with this question: "Art thou he that should come, or do we look for another?" His doubt was born of God's strange dealing with him.

3. There are those who doubt because of their willful disobedience. This, I am convinced, causes more doubt than all else. However little you may believe, if you live up to that little it will grow from more to more. But however strong your faith, if you become deliberately disloyal to that faith it will inevitably die. Here that word of Jesus is supremely true. "Unto every one that hath shall be given, and he shall have abundance: but from him that

hath not, shall be taken away even that which he hath."
The way to spiritual certainty is the way of obedience.
"If any man is willing to do his will, he shall know."

4. Finally, there are those who fall into doubt because
they become obsessed by their difficulties. This was the
cause of Simon's failure. He was getting on quite well
until he saw how boisterous the wind was. Then he took
his eyes off the Master and fixed them on the raging sea.
Looking at the storm he came to believe in its might more
than in the might of his Lord. He saw Jesus through his
difficulties instead of looking at his difficulties in the light
of his Lord. Thus his problems loomed so large that they
blinded him altogether to the presence of Christ.

This is an ever-present danger. It threatens us especially
today as we face our national problems. The clouds that
gather on the horizon of the world at present are very
black. So black are they that for multitudes they have
hidden the face of God. Many are so obsessed by their
dangers that they are blind to their advantages. They are
like the ten spies who went to spy out the Promised Land.
These became so keenly conscious of the giants that they
forgot utterly the leadership of their victorious Lord.

Just as this is true among the nations today, it is also
true of many of us individually. There are those who are
so obsessed by their personal difficulties that they can see
nothing else. Even when they go to pray they too often
fail to look to him who "is able to do exceeding abun-
dantly above all that we ask or think." They rather look
at their own weaknesses and pressing needs. Thus their
prayers often become a source of weakness rather than of

49

strength. Our one hope is to look to God. This is his word: "Look unto me, and be ye saved, all the ends of the earth."

IV

Even in his defeat Simon has a helpful message for us. Though he made a failure he did not allow his defeat to discourage him. He recovered his faith and ended in a triumph that thrills us to this hour. How did he do it?

1. He faced the facts about himself. When he found himself sinking he did not shut his eyes to that depressing fact. He did not try to bluff it through. He did not tell himself that while he was making a mess of things such failure was all he had a right to expect. He faced the fact that though Jesus had invited him, he was sinking right in his presence. Then he faced the further fact that he could not manage the situation alone. Simon faced these two facts: I am sinking; I cannot save myself.

2. Having faced the facts, Simon looked to him who is able to help. Simon took his eyes off the storm and fixed them again on Jesus. Then he prayed. I like his prayer. I like the intensity of it. I like the brevity of it. When we have no burden we can pray wordy prayers. But when we face a problem that is a matter of life or death, then we come to the point. This Simon did. He simply cried, "Lord, save me." Then what? Jesus saved him. That mighty hand that is always feeling for yours and mine in calm and in tempest, in the daylight and in the dark, gripped the uplifted hand of Simon and lifted him out of defeat into victory. So it may happen to us. Let us reach our hands to him in the faith that his hand is reaching for ours.

V

THE SUPREME QUESTION

"Who say ye that I am?"

MATTHEW 16:15

ex

JESUS had gone with his disciples to the district of Caesarea Philippi for a brief retirement. Here he asked this inner circle of friends two questions. The first of these questions had to do with the impression that he had made upon the people during his brief ministry. "Who do men say that I am?" he asked. I dare say that Jesus already knew the answer to this question quite as well as his friends. He was therefore not so much seeking information as he was seeking to help these friends to a clear and solid affirmation of their own faith.

In answering this question his disciples did not tell the whole story. They passed over the ugly criticisms that they had heard. They said nothing of those who had accused their Master of being a winebibber and a glutton and a friend of publicans and sinners. Instead, they told him only the complimentary things that they had heard. They declared that some had been so impressed by his fiery earnestness that they thought he might be John the Baptist come back from the dead. Others had felt the rugged strength of him and had called him Elijah. Others had been gripped by his tenderness and had named him Jeremiah. Others still, feeling that he embodied the very finest qualities of the heroes of the past, said that he was one of the old prophets.

This was the very climax of the complimentary. To be likened to a living prophet might be anything but flattering. Real prophets, while they are alive, generally manage to get themselves heartily hated. But to be likened to one of the great prophets long since dead was praise indeed. Yet Jesus heard these words of high commendation without the slightest enthusiasm. I dare say he was no more thrilled by them than he is thrilled today when we see in him only a personality so great that he cut history squarely in two.

We are accustomed to honor our illustrious dead. We celebrate the anniversaries of certain select souls whose achievements in point of character and conduct have been outstanding. We write books to remind ourselves of the virtues that made these great personalities what they were and to quicken our sense of gratitude for the high service they rendered. We impress upon our children a sense of obligation and responsibility to pass on to others the lighted torches that we have received from their hands. But when life grows hard and we find ourselves in the midst of bleak winter, none of us turn to George Washington in memory of his heroic struggle at Valley Forge. As much as we honor him, we do not seek help from him.

Those who think of Jesus as a great prophet are altogether right, but that is not enough. That answer aroused no enthusiasm in Jesus.

Having asked this question about other men's opinion, Jesus asked the disciples to speak for themselves. He put the question to them personally: "Who say ye that I am?"

This is a question to which we might well await the answer in breathless anticipation. Other men spoke from hearsay or from seeing Jesus once or twice. But these disciples are the star witnesses. They have been with him constantly. They have heard all his words; they have seen all his deeds. What is their answer?

When they first began to follow him, they had no clearly defined answer. They found him amazingly exciting. They found him by far the most winsome personality they had ever known. At times he shocked them. At times he thrilled them. At other times he filled them with awe and wonder. He set them whispering to each other, "What manner of man is this?" Whoever he was, they were sure that he was vastly greater than any other they had ever known.

Now the cross was only about six months away. The Master had taken them for a retreat to Caesarea Philippi. Evidently he thought that they had been with him long enough to have reached some definite conclusion. They had seen him in solitude and in the midst of crowds; they had been by when he had prayed, when he had preached, when he performed his works of wonder. So he now put to them this question, "Who say ye that I am?"

Impulsive Simon speaks up for them all. In a tremendous answer he affirms his faith: "Thou art the Christ, the Son of the living God." That is, Simon is saying, "I have found in thee the very values that I seek and that I find in God."

And what was the reaction of Jesus? Did he rebuke Simon, as any honest man who was mere man would have done? When a few years later Paul and Barnabas had created such enthusiasm in Lystra that the people were on the point of offering them sacrifices because they thought they were gods, what was the reaction of these good men? They were horrified. They repudiated such honor though it came very near to costing Paul his life.

But what, I repeat, was the reaction of Jesus to Simon's answer? He did not rebuke Simon. He rather pronounced a blessing upon him. With wholehearted enthusiasm he said: "Blessed art thou, Simon, Bar-jona: for flesh and blood hath not revealed it unto thee, but my Father which is in heaven." He thus declared that the conviction of Simon is the truth, a truth that he had come to possess because he had been illuminated by the very light of God.

"Thou art the Christ, the Son of the living God." That was no passing notion, no spur-of-the-moment guess later seen in another light. The certainty of Simon and his fellow disciples that Jesus is God come in the flesh did not weaken with the passing of the years, but rather grew stronger. Having witnessed the death and resurrection of their Master, and having experienced Pentecost, these men became aboslutely certain that the same Jesus with whom they had walked the roadways of Galilee was alive forevermore. They became certain that he was both with and within them as a living presence. Not only so, but

54

they became the kind of men and did the kind of deeds that we should expect God-possessed men to become and to accomplish.

I

Is the faith of these disciples your faith? Today Jesus is searching our hearts with this question: "Who say ye that I am?" This is an abiding question. In every age it is the most important question with which men have to deal. It is therefore the most important question that confronts you and me today. This is not simply my conviction; it is the conviction of Jesus himself. It is so important that if we give it a wrong answer, though if it were possible we might give a right answer to every other question, life must be an adventure of failure and of tragedy. It is so important that if we give it a right answer, though if it were possible we might give a wrong answer to every other question, life would still be an adventure of joy and victory.

Listen to these daring words of Jesus: "Whosoever heareth these sayings of mine, and doeth them, I will liken him unto a wise man, which built his house upon a rock. . . . And every one that heareth these sayings of mine, and doeth them not, shall be likened unto a foolish man, which built his house upon the sand." Thus does Jesus claim to be the arbiter of human destiny. He claims that whether nations or individuals rise or fall, survive or perish, depends upon their attitude toward him.

If you remind me that Jesus is here talking about his sayings, his teachings, and not about himself, I answer that Jesus and his teachings are one. He did not claim merely to teach the truth. He said: "I am . . . the truth." He himself is Christianity: Listen to him: "Blessed are they which are persecuted for righteousness' sake. . . . Blessed are ye, when men shall revile you, and persecute you, and shall say all manner of evil against you falsely, for my sake." "For righteousness' sake" and "for my sake" are synonymous. This is the case because Jesus is the very incarnation of righteousness. He and his teachings are one.

Recently a distinguished minister declared that in order to be a Christian it is only necessary to share the faith of Jesus. This faith he summed up as faith in a fatherly God and in the brotherhood of man. He asserted that our attitude toward Jesus himself is not of prime importance. However much truth there may be in that assertion, this I can say with absolute conviction: such is not the Christianity of the New Testament. It is not the Christianity possessed by the disciples, nor is it the Christianity taught by Jesus. The supreme question of the New Testament is not, "What think ye of the faith of Jesus?" but, "What think ye of Christ?" It is, "Who say ye that I am?"

How flatly this contradicts the conviction held by so many today—that what one believes is a matter of no great importance! There are still intelligent churchmen who are lukewarm in their attitude toward the missionary enterprises of the church because they are possessed of a hazy belief that one faith is about as good as another. Christianity may be good for Occidentals, but it might not work so well for those living in the Orient. Yet the law of gravitation works just as well for the one as for the other.

I read somewhere that a committee of Japanese waited on the philosopher Herbert Spencer years ago to discuss with him the wisdom of adopting a state religion for Japan. He thought that such a step might be wise. Then when they asked what religion they should adopt, he agreed that their own Shintoism, being a native religion, might be quite as good for them—if not better—as any other, not excepting Christianity.

Now, had a friend told Herbert Spencer after this interview that he had assisted in placing an infernal bomb under the Japanese nation that would one day blow it to bits and leave black wounds on the rest of the world, he would have heard him in utter incredulity. This would have been the case because Spencer was an unbeliever and looked upon one faith as about as good as another.

But regardless of what Spencer had to do with it, what actually came of the adopting of a religion on the part of Japan that taught that the emperor is divine? Multitudes took that creed seriously. Believing that they had the Son of Heaven for their emperor, they naturally came to believe that a people so highly favored were destined to rule the world. One who had lived long in Japan declared that when he would tell a Japanese friend that he did not share his faith that his nation was destined to conquer the world, this friend would not become angry; he would just be astonished that one should be so ignorant and illogical. Thus the attack on Pearl Harbor, the fanatical heroism with which the Japanese fought, was the natural outcome of their faith. What they believed wrecked them and caused them to seek to wreck the world.

The greatest threat to modern civilization today, in my opinion, is atheistical communism. What is wrong with the Communist? It is not that he by nature differs from ourselves. If you were to prick him, he would bleed. He is not made of the slime and ooze of things while we are made of far finer material. Yet here is a man who acknowledges no loyalty except that to his political party. There is no other trust that he will not betray. There is not a crime that he is not ready to commit. Why is this the case? It is because of what he believes.

What one believes, therefore, is a matter of great importance. This is the case because beliefs are creative. As a wrong faith issues in wrong character and wrong conduct, even so a right faith issues in right character and right conduct. Therefore when Jesus searches us with this question, "Who say ye that I am?" he is asking a question of supreme importance. Upon the answer we give to that question depends the destiny of the individual and the destiny of the world.

II

"Who say ye that I am?" That question is intensely personal.

Some time ago a friend of mine sent a manuscript to his publisher. It happens that this friend is a great reader. In writing his book he seems to have said to himself: "Why should I read so widely and not use what I have read?" Therefore he fairly crowded his manuscript with quotations. The result was that it was returned a few weeks later with this notation: "Too many quotations. We want to know what you think."

When Paul reached Rome as a prisoner, his fellow Jews gathered about him to hear what he had to say. "We know," they declared, "that this sect to which you belong is everywhere spoken against. You Christians have a bad reputation. But we desire to know what you think. Evidently," they seemed to say, "something big has happened to you. Something has brought you through. Tell us what you think of the Christ whose you are and whom you serve. Who do you say that he is?"

In the same way I bring this question to your own heart and mine. Who do you say that Jesus is? I am happy in the conviction that there are those who find in him just what these early saints found. He is to many of you a "friend that sticketh closer than a brother." He is your Lord and Master, your personal Saviour. You too can sing:

> "Thou, O Christ, art all I want;
> More than all in thee I find."

For those of you who have not come to this bracing certainty I have this good news. You too may give a satisfying answer to this question out of your own experience. You too can say: "I know whom I have believed, and am persuaded that he is able to keep that which I have committed unto him against that day." Certainly that is a consummation devoutly to be wished.

Christianity is a religion of giving—worldly goods, time, talents, love, our very selves. But it is also a religion of receiving. When God gave himself in the person of Jesus Christ in that distant day, some refused to receive the gift. Here is one of the saddest sentences ever written: "He came unto his own, and his own received him not." But there were those who did receive him. That sad sentence is followed by one of the most thrilling ever written: "As many as received him, to them gave he power to become." That is what Jesus is constantly doing for those who receive him. He gives them the power to become. Simon received power to become a rock of Christlike character. Fanatical and narrow John received power to become an apostle of love. To all he gives power to become new creations in Christ Jesus.

Receiving him, we not only receive power to become Christlike, but we also receive power to give somewhat as he gave. There were those in that distant day who declared, "We have no king but Caesar." Built upon that foundation, their houses were swept into oblivion long centuries ago. There was a far smaller group who went out saying, "We have no king but Christ." These still enrich us, these still breathe upon us like the breath of an eternal springtime. Receiving power to live, they also received power to give. So it may be for us.

I think about the most needlessly cruel deed I ever witnessed took place at a Christmas celebration in our little village church. The tree must have been quite a crude affair, but to my boyish eyes it had the beauty of paradise. Santa Claus was present in person. We boys and girls gathered about him while he called our names and filled our hands with presents.

But there was one boy whose name was not called. He was the village idiot. He stood with his ugly face turned toward the tree, one gaunt wistfulness. Then Santa Claus took down the largest box that was on the tree and called his name. He reached for his present with eager hands. He untied the string with fingers that trembled. Then he lifted the lid to find the box empty. Somebody, mistaking a tragedy for a joke, had given him only an empty box.

We are hanging presents upon the world's great Christmas tree, each of us. The presents we hang are the lives we live. Some give lives that are empty of goodness and empty of God. But it need not be so. It will certainly not be so for him who shares the faith of the disciples that Jesus is "the Christ, the Son of the living God" and receives this Christ into his own heart. This is the case because "he that believeth on me, . . . out of his inner life shall flow rivers of living water."

"Who say ye that I am?" To answer that question aright is to receive power to live and power to give.

VI

BREAD

*"Why reason ye, because ye have no bread?
... Do ye not remember?"*

MARK 8:17-18

୧∼୬

DO ye not remember?" This question was born of
pained amazement. Jesus was finding it difficult to
be patient with his blundering disciples. When he warned
them to beware of the leaven of the Pharisees they missed
the point altogether. They failed to understand that his
warning was against the doctrine of the Pharisees. The
word "leaven" had misled them. They saw in that word
nothing but bread. Therefore when they took account of
their assets and found that they had only one loaf, they
were in a perfect fever of anxiety.

Now it was this anxiety on the part of his disciples
that filled the Master with pained amazement. He could
not see, in the light of their own experiences, how they
could be so worried about bread. Since he had met their
needs in the past, they should have trusted him to meet
them in the future. Thus it was not a too great interest in

bread on the part of these disciples that disturbed Jesus, but rather their lack of faith. The Master is not here minimizing the importance of bread, as a surface reading of the story might suggest. He is rather magnifying its importance. He is seeking to teach his disciples that he is both willing and able to supply all our needs. Therefore he questions: "Do ye not remember?" What then are we to remember?

I

We are to remember the interest of our Lord in those needs that we are accustomed to call physical and temporal. He knows that man cannot live by bread alone. He also knows that man cannot live without bread. He is therefore as truly interested in the bread that gives life to the body as he is in the bread that gives life to the soul. Our failure to realize this has led to a conviction regarding Jesus that has resulted in untold harm. That conviction is that Jesus is not quite practical. His teachings are of course unspeakably beautiful. He is indeed "the sweet Galilean dreamer." If we only lived in castles in the air, or if we were souls without any bodies, then his teachings might be excellent. But since we have bodies that must be housed and clothed and fed, we had better look elsewhere for teaching that fits us to live the life that now is.

But this view is flatly contradictory to the teaching of Jesus. Our Lord is interested in all our interests. He never drew any sharp distinction between the secular and the sacred as we are accustomed to do. When a housewife makes a cake she does not put the sugar in one compartment and the other ingredients in another. The sugar permeates the whole cake. Thus with Jesus religion permeated the whole of life. He knew that for one to be religious on holy days and in holy places was not in reality to be religious at all. Jesus therefore was interested in the temporal as well as the spiritual.

Since this is the case, our Lord never concerned himself merely about the souls of men. I do not read that he ever asked any man: "How is your soul?" Of course he knew that man is both body and spirit. But he was interested not in bodies and not in spirits. He was interested in folks; in men and women, boys and girls. He knew that while man is both a son of Adam and a son of God, he is also a unit. What therefore God had joined together he did not put asunder. He was interested in the whole man.

Jesus realized, I am sure, something of the tremendous influence of the mind over the body. We are told today that some 60 per cent of those occupying beds in our hospitals became ill mentally before they were ill physically. A sick mind is very likely to eventuate in a sick body.

But if the mind influences the body, so does the body influence the mind. This body is the house in which I live. If it comes to be a tumble-down ruin, I may still be sound in my soul, but such an achievement will not be easy. Other things being equal, it is far easier to be genuinely Christian with a sound body than with one that is tortured by disease. It is easier to be sunny and optimistic when we feel fit than when we feel unfit.

We recognize this every day by the apologies we make, both for ourselves and others. When one we love is rude we say "he is not himself today." Even on the radio we hear one rail out in anger and then apologize by laying his loss of temper on a headache. Personally I have little respect for such excuses. I am exceedingly selfish if, just because I am miserable, I seek to make everybody about me miserable too. But when we do become peevish and fretful we often plead our pain for an excuse. Even so great a man as Thomas Carlyle sought to explain his years of snarling by saying nothing better could be expected of one who had dyspepsia gnawing like a rat at the pit of his stomach.

Elijah was a tremendous man. Both by nature and by grace he was one of the greatest of the prophets. But in spite of his greatness we find him one day whining and complaining like a spoiled child. He tells God frankly that he has had enough, that he wants to die. Great saint that he is, he is not even honest. He did not really wish to die. Had that been his desire he would not have had to pray about it. All he would have needed to have done would have been to stop over in Jezreel for a day or two. Jezebel would have fixed him up without any prayer. Why then is he thus playing the baby? It is in part because he is physically and nervously exhausted. Therefore the first step God took toward bringing him to himself was to feed him and give him a good night's sleep.

Since our Lord is concerned with the whole man he is keenly interested in bread. This interest runs through his entire ministry. When he passed through a wheat field with his disciples one Sabbath and these disciples gathered a bit of the grain to eat, the Pharisees were outraged. But the Master defended his offending friends both from scripture and common sense. Having cited the example of David he uttered this word of wisdom: "The Sabbath was made for man, and not man for the Sabbath." By this he was not minimizing the importance of the Sabbath. The Sabbath is of vast importance. But he was saying that no institution is so important as to be above human need. Then, in the passage of which our text is a part, Jesus reminds us that on two occasions he met the physical needs of the multitudes that gathered about him.

Just as our Lord was concerned about bread in the days of his flesh, so was he concerned after his resurrection. Listen to this winsome story. A little group of disciples who have been fishing are coming home in the gloaming of early morning. They see a stranger on the shore. Then this stranger speaks: "Lads, have you caught anything?" When they answer that they have caught nothing he tells them how to cast their net in order to be successful. Then when they reach the shore they find breakfast waiting for them. Who prepared it? Their risen Lord. How wonderful that those mighty hands that created the universe, those hands that had just throttled death and the grave, were not above the lowly task of getting breakfast for a few tired fishermen who had just come in from a night of toil. Remember that our Lord is interested in all our needs. That means that he is interested in bread.

II

We need to remember that bread is God's gift. When Jesus taught us to pray he taught us this petition: "Give us this day our daily bread." It seems to me significant too that he told us to ask for bread before we ask for forgiveness, as important as that is. We are to pray for bread before we pray for victory over temptation. This is the case because Jesus knew that we are not apt to be greatly concerned about forgiveness if we are being tortured by hunger. He knew that we are not likely to pray very earnestly not to be led into temptation if starving children are tugging at us asking for bread that we cannot give. We are to ask for bread because all bread comes from God.

It is not always easy to realize this in our land of plenty. It is far easier for us to realize our dependence upon God for the bread of life than it is for us to realize our dependence upon him for material bread. Of course the bread of life is a gift. "The wages of sin is death; but the gift of God is eternal life through Jesus Christ our Lord." But we save ourselves spiritually quite as easily as we can save ourselves physically. All the scientists of all the centuries could no more create a loaf of bread in independence of God than they could create a universe.

"Remember," Jesus might urge, "that I am interested in bread, and that all bread comes from God." To fail to realize this is not the part of wisdom but of folly. Why was the rich farmer a fool? For a number of reasons, this among them: He thought because he had barns filled to overflowing that he could get on without God. But every man must lean upon God for the supply of every physical need. Even the fact that bread can meet our physical needs is a mystery. The fact that the same loaf could give strength to Judas for treachery and to Jesus for bearing his cross is a mystery. Both bread and its power to give life come from God's hands. Remember then that bread is God's gift.

III

We are to remember that God gives bread as we co-operate with him and with each other. This feeding of the five thousand was a co-operative enterprise. All successful dealings with the bread question must be so.

1. To produce bread we must co-operate with God. My father was a Christian farmer. He was a man of prayer. He prayed about all his needs, but when the spring came he did not ask God to plant corn in one field and to sow oats in another. He had me to do that. He knew that the cultivation and reaping of a harvest was a matter of co-operation between man and God.

2. Not only must man co-operate with God, but he must co-operate with his brother. When Jesus taught us to pray for bread he taught us to say "give us," and not merely "give me." If therefore I am an employer, when I pray this prayer, if I pray it intelligently and sinecrely, I am asking for bread not simply for myself, but for the man who works for me and with me. Therefore I will help to answer my prayer by paying a living wage. Even so, if I am an employee and pray this prayer, I am asking bread not for myself alone, but for my employer. I will therefore do an honest day's work. How much precious bread has been wasted because of a lack of co-operation between employer and employee!

This is also a prayer for the nations. How many wasteful wars have been fought primarily over the bread question! For us in rich America to help the devastated nations of the world is good religion. It is far more than good religion; it is sound economics. One group cannot have an abundance, and the other be tortured by want, without tragedy. Jesus gave some stern warnings of the perils of refusing to share. On the surface these warnings may sound arbitrary, but in reality they are not. They are true in the nature of things.

Look, for instance, at the picture of the Last Judgment. To one group the King says: "Depart from me, ye cursed." To the other: "Come, ye blessed of my Father." Why this difference? Why was the one group turned away while the other was made welcome? The charge against the group that was banished was in part this: "I was an hungred, and ye gave me no meat." The commendation of those who were welcomed into everlasting life was this: "I was an hungred, and ye gave me meat." It would seem therefore that our heaven or hell depends on our willingness to share our daily bread.

Here is another story that, if possible, seems even more stern. "There was a certain rich man, which was clothed in purple and fine linen, and fared sumptuously every day: and there was a certain beggar named Lazarus, which was laid at his gate, full of sores, and desiring to be fed with the crumbs which fell from the rich man's table: moreover the dogs came and licked his sores. And it came to pass, that the beggar died, and was carried by the angels into Abraham's bosom: the rich man also died and was buried; and in hell he lift up his eyes."

What was the sin of this rich man? It was not that he set the dogs on this helpless beggar. It was not that he had him stoned. He rather allowed him to die of neglect. Therefore in hell he lifted up his eyes. Are we then to understand that to refuse to share our bread means that in the afterlife we shall be cast into hell? About that I cannot speak with authority. But what is certain is that such failure means that we shall be cast into hell in the here and now. That is not theory; that is experience. It is what has taken place over and over again. It will continue to take place until we become Christian in our attitude toward bread.

IV

Now suppose we do remember. Suppose we take Jesus seriously when he tells us that he is concerned about bread, that bread is his gift, and that he can only give it to us when we co-operate with him and with our fellows, what happens?

1. Such an attitude brings a sense of God into our daily lives. The earning of our daily bread becomes a beautiful and sacred task. It enables us to handle the tools of our trade as religiously as we handle our Bibles and our hymnbooks on Sunday morning.

2. To take Jesus seriously means that every meal becomes a sacrament. When Cleopas and his companion were going home after the crucifixion they were utterly heartbroken. But a winsome stranger joined them. This

70

stranger so charmed them by his conversation that they almost forget their sorrow. When they reached the door of their humble little home they felt that they could not let this companion go on his way: "Abide with us," they urged, "for it is toward evening, and the day is far spent."

Their urgent invitation was accepted. Soon supper was announced. Then what? "And it came to pass, as he sat at meat with them, he took bread and blessed it, and brake, and gave to them. And their eyes were opened, and they knew him." The risen Christ was known to them in the breaking of bread. We too may so see the finger marks of our Lord upon our bread that every meal will become a sacrament.

3. Finally, this taking of our Lord seriously in the matter of bread is a fundamental step, not only toward the saving of our bodies and our souls, but of our civilization as well. To look on bread as a gift from God to be earned and shared in co-operation with him and with our fellows is a necessity for right living. This also is the one way of preventing the ghastly waste, both in bread and blood, that the past centuries have witnessed. Shall we not remember?

VII

PROFIT AND LOSS

"What shall it profit a man, if he shall gain the whole world, and lose his own soul?"

MARK 8:36

❧

JESUS was never interested in winning disciples whose loyalty was born of blindness or lack of understanding. When a young man came to him one day all aflame with enthusiasm vowing: "I will follow thee whithersoever thou goest," the Master did not respond with a kindred enthusiasm. He saw that this eager volunteer did not understand what discipleship involved. Therefore he quenched the fires of his youthful ardor with this dash of cold water: "The foxes have holes, and the birds of the air have nests; but the Son of man hath not where to lay his head."

Sometime ago I gave myself the trouble of boarding a train when I did not know where the train was going. I thought it was going to Washington, D. C., but I found that it was headed for Washington, N. C. When my mistake was discovered I had to get off and walk about a mile back to the station carrying two heavy grips. Not only that, but by taking the wrong train I missed the right one. Our Lord urges that we count the cost, that we know where the train is going before we get on board. Therefore he arrests us with the question: "What shall it profit a man, if he shall gain the whole world, and lose his own soul?"

I

This text sounds a bit old-fashioned, but it has in it one word that is thoroughly up-to-date. In fact, this word is quite as much at home in our day as when it was uttered nearly two thousand years ago. That word is "profit"— "What shall it profit a man?" Everybody is interested in profits of one kind or another, and rightly so. This therefore is a sane question that we may ask either selfishly or unselfishly. It is perfectly right to ask it. The tragedy is that so many ask it with an eye only for one kind of profit, that which is of the earth earthy.

Years ago, as an enthusiastic young teacher, I sought to erect a new high-school building in the village where I was teaching. To this end I invited some of the leading citizens of the town to a meeting. When I had outlined my plan, one of them, the wealthiest of the group, said: "I am all for it if you will show me the dividends." By this he meant that he was willing to help construct the new building provided I could show him how it would pay him in dollars and cents. The dividends that it would pay in terms of better trained boys and girls and better citizens did not interest him in the least. He was interested in financial returns and those only.

73

One of the most crucial problems of our day is the liquor problem. We are on the way to becoming the drunkest nation on the face of the earth. What makes liquor a problem? It is made so by two classes of people. Eliminate these and liquor will be no more a problem than sassafras tea. The first class is composed of those who desire to drink liquor. Some of these are quite decent and respectable people who are in search of a thrill. Some are seeking momentary escape from the dull monotony of life or from a sense of inferiority. Then there are those who are in bondage to liquor and have become such hopeless slaves that they are willing to pay any price for a drink.

The second group, the one in my opinion that is far the more dangerous and selfish and wicked, is made up of those who are bent on making money out of liquor. These manufacture it, sell it, rent their property for its sale, vote for it, all in order to gain financial profit. Naturally these have no desire to make drunkards; they have no joy in robbing children of their chances or in sending a father staggering down the street to make a hell of his home. But they are willing to run the risk of doing this in order to make money. Take the profit motive out of liquor and I am sure this deadly evil could soon be brought under control.

Sad to say, there is no crime that men have not been willing to commit in an effort to win worldly gain. This question therefore may be asked selfishly, but it may also be asked unselfishly. There is a profit that we cannot measure in terms of dollars and cents. Here, for instance, is a lonely man in the heart of Africa. He has had one attack of fever after another. Because he is suffering from scurvy he is having to knock his own teeth out one by one. Why does David Livingstone not go home where he can keep his health? What is he seeking to gain by his mad adventure? He is out after profit. He is seeking the profit that comes from helping to heal the world's open sore. He is seeking profit for others rather than for himself. By so doing he is being vastly enriched.

Now these are the two kinds of profit between which we are to choose. Of course we often choose now one and then the other. But at long last there is one that we make central, one that we put first. Jesus sums up these two types of profit in two words: the world and the soul. "What shall it profit a man, if he shall gain the whole world, and lose his own soul?"

What is the world? It is all in the way of fame and fortune that our present dwelling place has to offer. Of course the world in itself is not an ugly and evil thing. It is beautiful and desirable. God himself called it very good. The world only becomes an evil when it ceases to be a servant and becomes a master. As a master it stands for that spirit of self-pleasing that is so prevalent today and everyday. To choose the world therefore is to seek to please ourselves, to save our own lives, to be independent toward God.

Jesus indicated this in his reply to Peter. The Master has just declared that he must suffer and be rejected and be killed. But Peter cannot stand for this, so he took him and began to rebuke him saying in effect: "Be it far from thee, Lord. What is the use in having power if you do not capitalize on it for yourself?" At this the Master turned upon Peter saying: "Get thee behind me, Satan. . . . Thou savourest not the things that be of God, but those that be of men." In other words: "You are talking the language of the world, you are not talking the language of God."

The other value offered for our choice is the soul. This word is also translated "life." Of course life as here used does not mean mere length of days. A man might exist for a century and never really live for a single hour. No more is this life a product of things. "A man's life consisteth not in the abundance of the things which he possesseth." To save the soul is to come into possession of values that are moral and spiritual. It is a quality of life that becomes ours when we surrender wholeheartedly to Jesus Christ. The salvation of the soul is the natural outcome of a vital faith in God.

II

What is involved in our choice of the world? What do we promise ourselves if we put the world first?

Our gain in terms of material values is uncertain. We may gain very little or we may gain very much. For the sake of argument, Jesus assumes that we may gain everything. He is assuming that by putting the world first we shall succeed in winning all that it has to offer. Of course nobody has ever really done that. Vast multitudes who have put it first have won exceedingly little.

But over against this uncertainty of worldly gain there is a certainty of tragic loss. The man who puts the world first will surely lose his soul. That fact ought to give us pause. There is such a thing as losing the soul. It is possible for a nation to lose its soul. It is possible also for an individual. One calls attention to the fact that when H. G. Wells was on his deathbed he answered a friend in this fashion: "Do not bother me. Don't you see I am busy dying." Busy dying! That is an arresting word. In recent years we have seen nations exceedingly busy doing just that. We have seen individuals doing the same. I visited a man sometime ago who gave me the impression that he was doing just that. As I came from that interview I said to my companion: "He impresses me as a man who is slowly rotting down." He was busy dying.

Now this loss of the soul is the supreme and all-inclusive loss. There are lesser losses that might give us pause. What shall it profit a man if he gain the whole world and lose his health? Many a man does just that. But how much in terms of material values would you charge to become a physical wreck? What would be the gain of being able to buy the daintiest of food, but be too sick to eat it; to have the money to buy the choicest of cars, but be too sick to ride in them; to possess the most comfortable beds and yet be utterly restless?

What would it profit a man to gain the whole world and lose his physical life? Many a man has paid this price for an insignificant fraction of the world, though few have paid it deliberately. In the backwoods community where I lived as a boy there was a man who had worked like a slave and lived a bit like a pig. Thus he managed to accumulate some $5,000 in gold. He would not trust it to a bank, but kept it hidden in his cabin. One night a high-wayman paid him a visit, and, putting his gun so close to the miser's face that he could almost smell the powder, asked him for a donation. The miser responded to that appeal by giving the highwayman all that he had. The next day an old friend came to condole with him.

"Homer, he asked, "did you give him all the money you had?"

"Yes," came the answer, "every bit of it."

"Why did you not argue with him?" the friend continued.

"Argue with him?" came the indignant question. "Argue with him? Hell was too close." He loved money, but he did not love it well enough to die for it.

Here is one who even did that. Nearly a century ago a boat whose passenger list was made up mainly of miners returning from the gold fields of California was making its way up the Mississippi. Suddenly that boat struck an obstruction that tore a great wound in its hull. At once it began rapidly to sink. There were not enough lifeboats, so many of the miners, seeing that they must swim for their lives, unfastened their belts heavy with gold and threw them on the deck of the boat. But there was one miner who thought these were mad. He therefore gathered up the belts one by one and fastened them upon himself. Thus hampered he jumped into the water and sank as if he had been made of lead. They found his body a few days later, but no one congratulated him upon his vast wealth.

Now to lose one's soul is infinitely more than the loss of

physical life. There are treasures for which one might gladly die. But for me to lose my soul is to lose my very self. It means the loss of all of my finest possibilities. It means the loss of the privilege of Christlike character. It means the loss of all those values that come from faith in God. For such a loss there is absolutely no compensation. The man who loses his soul loses his all.

This is equally true of a nation. The nation that loses its soul always ends by losing itself. When we hold an autopsy over the once-mighty nations that are dead today how do we find that they came by their death? They were not destroyed by outside enemies. They did not starve for physical bread. They starved for the bread of life. The nation that loses God loses its soul. The secular nation, as the secular man, is not headed toward life, but toward death. Woodrow Wilson was right when he affirmed that a nation cannot be materially secure unless it is spiritually redeemed.

III

Now suppose we make the high choice, the choice of life. Suppose instead of seeking merely to save ourselves, we give ourselves in wholehearted surrender to God. Then what?

1. If we put God first in our seeking we are sure to find him. As we give ourselves to God he gives himself to us. This is not theory. This is experience. If everyone who has found this true were to say "Amen," it would boom like a cannonade and shake like an earthquake. "If any man is willing to do his will, he shall know."

79

2. In finding God we shall find all that life needs. "Seek ye first the kingdom of God, and his righteousness; and all these things shall be added unto you." Jesus in saying this is speaking to the group rather than to the individual. There is no doubt that the man who puts God first, generally speaking, has a better chance at things than the man who does not. But if there are those who would question that putting God first would guarantee that all our material needs would be met, this certainly does apply to society as a whole.

3. Finding God, we shall not only have our physical needs met, but we shall find satisfaction for the highest hungers of the heart. "If any man thirst," says Jesus, "let him come unto me, and drink." He has that to give without which we die. All our highest hungers, all our deepest thirsts, are met in him. "My God shall supply all your need according to his riches in glory by Christ Jesus."

Then everybody at his best desires to be useful. We cannot but realize the deep tragedy of missing the majesty and the mirth of being helpful to our fellows. This need is also supplied by our Lord. "He that believeth on me, as the scripture hath said, from within him shall flow rivers of living water." (A.S.V.) Thus putting Christ first we find satisfaction for ourselves. We also have something to share. Out of our inner lives "shall flow rivers of living water." We shall have power to break up the drought of the soul and to set the fields of the heart to flowering.

"What shall it profit a man, if he shall gain the whole world, and lose his own soul?" It is a choice between self-seeking and self-giving, between those values that are of the earth earthy, and of those values that are born of a vital faith in God. You have just one life to invest. Where are you going to invest it? Are you going to stake your all on a spiritual interpretation of life or a material one? Will you put yourself first, or God first?

One day I stopped and watched some young ants coming up out of the ground. They spread their silvery wings in the sunlight as if they were made for the skyland and the upper air. But before I could be thrilled over their beautiful destiny, they seemed to say to themselves: "Business is business, I cannot waste my time developing and using my wings." So they laid them quickly aside and went to the practical business of crawling.

Schiller tells this story. Once the bird had no wings. They merely walked about in the dust having no commerce with the sky at all. Then one day the Lord threw wings at their feet and commanded them to pick them up and carry them for his sake. At first it seemed very hard. They thought they were going to have a heavy handicap. But in obedience they held the wings close to their sides, and the wings grew. At last what they had once thought would be only a hampering weight lifted them into the heights. We can take the way of the ants or the birds. As we seek for ourselves we lose our wings. As we give ourselves we are able to mount up with wings as eagles. What is your choice?

VIII

BEING DECISIVE

"Why call ye me, Lord, Lord, and do not the things which I say?"

LUKE 6:46

❧

THIS sane question is addressed to the undecided. In speaking to you on being decisive I am speaking on a subject of major importance. This is an essential for successful living. If you know where you are going and are determined to get there, almost any old jalopy will serve the purpose. But if you cannot come to a definite decision as to your goal, then a Rolls-Royce will be of little avail. It would wear out and fall to pieces before you would reach your goal. Truly, for the ship that is bound for no harbor no wind can be favorable. No wonder therefore that our Lord is constantly calling us to be decisive: "Let your language be, 'Yes, yes,' or 'No, no.'" (Weymouth.)

How essential that is, and yet how difficult! So often our "Yes" has in it a tincture of "No," and our "No" a tincture of "Yes." To give utterance to a "Yes" that is 100 per cent affirmation is about the most difficult task that we are called upon to perform. The burden of choice is so heavy that many people go to pieces under it. There are young men who were happier in the army than they have ever been before or since. This is the case because there they were in some measure relieved of the burden of choice.

It is difficult to get people to think. It is more difficult still to get them to be decisive. What a keen thinker was Hamlet, Prince of Denmark! There are those who believe that the story of this prince is somewhat autobiographical. They believe that Hamlet, with his vast ability to think and his inability to act, is in a measure a picture of the poet himself. Be that as it may, Hamlet found action next to impossible. He did not like his situation. He rebelled at the fact that his world was out of joint and that he was ever born to set it right. He contemplated suicide, thought of it with brilliant clearness, but could never quite decide to go through with it.

> "Who would fardels bear,
> To grunt and sweat under a weary life,
> But that the dread of something after death,
> The undiscover'd country from whose bourn
> No traveller returns, puzzles the will
> And makes us rather bear those ills we have
> Than fly to others that we know not of?
> Thus conscience does make cowards of us all;
> And thus the native hue of resolution
> Is sicklied o'er with the pale cast of thought,
> And enterprises of great pith and moment
> With this regard their currents turn awry,
> And lose the name of action."

I

Now look at this question of Jesus: "Why call ye me, Lord, Lord, and do not the things which I say?" We can readily realize the kind of folks to whom this question was addressed. Our Lord is not speaking to those who are out and out against him. He is not speaking to his avowed enemies, nor to those who ignore him. Neither is he speaking to those who are wholeheartedly for him. He is rather speaking to people very like many of us. He is speaking to those who admire him, who honor him to the point of calling him Lord, and yet who are not fully persuaded to follow him. They give him an intellectual assent, but have failed wholeheartedly to give him themselves.

Mark tells us of a man of this type. One day this man came to Jesus with this question: "Which is the first commandment of all?" When Jesus answered that the greatest commandment is to love God and man, his questioner approved his answer. In fact, he gave the answer of the Master such wise approval that Jesus commended him for his answer and then paid him this compliment: "Thou art not far from the kingdom of God." It was a beautiful commendation, and yet it was not enough. Though so near the kingdom that his foot was almost upon the threshold, he was not in it. One decisive step would have brought him to life's finest adventure, but so far as we know, he failed to take that step.

Now this company of the undecided is a vast company. It is not uncharitable to say that it includes a large percentage of the members of our churches. This does not mean that these undecided folks are hypocritical. Very few of them are. It does not mean that they do not refrain from certain evils every day out of loyalty to Christ. It does not mean that they do not do certain deeds of service every day because of that loyalty. It does mean that while they are obedient in many things, they still do not put the Kingdom of God first. Though decent, religious, and respectable, there are areas in their lives that they have never dedicated to him whom they call Lord.

Not only does this company of the undecided include vast numbers who are in our churches, but it includes even more who are outside any church. As I have spoken to various clubs and organizations outside the church I have discovered that it is by no means unpopular before such groups to sound a definitely religious note. Any reference to Jesus Christ, any word honoring him, is met with almost universal approval. Also as I have spoken to men individually who were outside the church I have found plenty of those who were harshly critical. These were often critical of the ministry. They could point out numerous flaws both in the church as a whole and in the individual members. But when I confessed that we were a faulty group all of us, and then asked this question, "What about Jesus Christ? What fault have you to find in him?" I do not recall ever to have heard from these one harsh criticism. In spite of all our faults, there is a sense in which Jesus Christ is the most popular character in the United States today. Our tragedy is not that we are out and out against him; it is rather than we are not out and out for him.

II

"Why call ye me, Lord, Lord, and do not the things which I say?" Now what is he asking at our hands? Let us get away from what is incidental to what is really essential.

To begin negatively Jesus is not asking primarily for our church membership. By this I do not mean that it is not the duty of every Christian to belong to some church. I realize that there are many decent and right-thinking people outside the church. But it is my conviction that those who take Jesus seriously will join some church. The church at the time of Jesus was even more faulty than the church of today, yet Jesus did not stand apart from it and stone it. He rather attended it as a matter of habit and conviction. He knew that what help he brought he must bring as a member of the church and not as an outside antagonist.

Here and there I find people who have become too pious to belong to any church. I was preaching to a congregation some years ago in which was a brother who was giving me most encouraging backing by his hearty amens. Now I approve of saying amen. When a hearer makes such a response I feel he is on my side. But this man overdid it. He was talking almost as fast as I was. By this I knew I had not yet rebuked his particular sin.

Then it happened. I said: "I believe in the church."

"Amen," was the response.

"Now and then," I continued, "I have found people who were too good to belong to any church."

"Amen."

"If I lived next door to a man like that," I continued, "I would lock my garage every night."

He started to say amen and it slid off like a feather-edged shingle. When the sermon was over I learned the truth. He had quit the church because the Lord had said: "Come out from among them and be ye separate." Personally I believe that if you take Jesus seriously you will join some church. But our Lord is not asking for that first of all.

No more is Jesus asking first for our work. Of course if we are in earnest about following him we are certain to do something about it. But his first demand is not for our work. Neither is he seeking first for our money. Naturally if our Christianity is real we shall be glad to give, but money does not come first. No more is our Lord asking for some kind of emotional response. He is seeking neither for our laughter nor our tears. For what then, I repeat, is he asking? He is asking for ourselves. He is saying to us what he said to Matthew long ago: "Follow me." This publican was decisive. He at once left all, rose up, and followed. This also we are to do. Jesus is asking what Paul urged in these words: "Present your bodies a living sacrifice." He is asking for our complete and unconditional dedication of life. Nothing less than that will meet his demands.

If you think that sounds difficult I am ready to agree. Jesus never hinted that discipleship was easy. But when he set out to redeem us he did not seek an easy way. He took the way of the cross. "This is my body," he declares, "which is given for you." "This," he is saying, "is my-

self, my very all, my everything, and it is given for you."
He asks that in return we take our discipleship seriously.
As he gave his all, we are to give our all. We are to say
day by day: "Not my will but thine be done."

III

Why should we do this?

1. We ought to be wholehearted in our decision because nothing else will satisfy our Lord. He is never
pleased with half-hearted devotion. In fact, it would
seem, as we turn the pages of the New Testament, that
that is just the attitude that he hates most. He even
prefers out-and-out antagonism. "I would thou wert cold
or hot." What are we here to do? Not to win success
primarily. Certainly we are not here to fail. We are here
to do the will of God. It is only by a wholehearted dedication to him that we can please him and thus fulfill God's
purpose for our lives.

2. It is only by our wholehearted loyalty that we can
find satisfaction for ourselves. There is no peace for the
undecided. The most wretched hours of our lives are those
hours when we are unable to reach a decision. Even a
wrong decision brings more peace than does indecision.
The wise story of Jonah emphasizes this fact.

Listen to this: "The word of the Lord came unto Jonah
... saying, Arise, go to Nineveh, that great city, and cry
against it." There were two possibilities open to this
prophet: to go or not to go. He decided against the call of
God. We have that amazing power. Having reached a
definite decision to renounce God by disobeying him, he

went on shipboard and fell fast asleep. The days and nights that had preceded his decision had been full of agony. When he at last decided, even though his decision was wrong, that decision brought sufficient peace to make sleep possible.

But the trouble with the peace born of a wrong decision is that it will not last. This is the case because God simply will not let us alone. He refuses to leave off his loving efforts to win us. "No man can be as bad as he wants to be." We may reject the high calling of God, but our rejection will bring us no permanent peace. It is only when we have fully committed ourselves to God that we come to know the peace that abides.

Then a wholehearted decision to follow Christ brings peace because so many lesser questions are decided by it. There are those for whom no moral issue is finally decided. Every morning they must decide whether they will pray or not pray, whether they will look into God's Word or neglect it. Every Sunday church attendance is an open question. These people are therefore in constant conflict. They remind one of that old story of the man who possessed a dog whose tail was far too long, but desiring to give the dog the least possible pain, he decided to cut it off an inch a day rather than all at once. If you take Jesus seriously a thousand lesser decisions will then be made in advance.

Not only will this one great decision include many that are smaller, but it will make every other right decision easier. The choice you made today was born quite largely of the choice you made yesterday. Every wrong choice makes the next wrong choice the easier and the surer. When Rip Van Winkle used to swear off drinking he would return to his bottle saying: "I will not count this one." But even if he failed to count it his weakened will did not. It chalked that failure against him. Now just as every wrong choice makes the next wrong choice easier, even so every right choice makes the next right choice easier and surer. We can so cultivate our right choices in the fellowship of Jesus that they become all but spontaneous.

3. Then we ought to be fully decided in the matter of following Christ, because this alone brings us to our highest usefulness. Indecision means weakness. Years ago when we were boys, my brother and I in passing through the fields had to cross a spring branch which was normally two or three feet wide. But heavy rains had given this little stream a breadth of from ten to fifteen feet. In spite of this we decided we could jump it. I was to adventure first. So I gave myself a good running start and was on the way to victory when my brother changed his mind and shouted, "Stop! Stop! Stop!" The result was that I lost my decisiveness. The further result was that I landed in the middle of the stream. But my failure was not due to my lack of athletic ability. It was due rather to my indecision.

In those dark days when Israel was being swept off its feet by Jezebel, it was Elijah who saved the day. Standing before a great throng he flung at them this sane question: "How long halt ye between two opinions?" In other words: "How long are you going to allow yourselves to be crippled by your indecision?" To be thus undecided is as silly as trying to win a foot race with a ball and chain on your ankle. Indecision brings weakness. Decision brings strength.

Years ago I watched a company of men move the side of a mountain. They were not using bulldozers as we do today. They were using hydraulic pressure. When that water fell from the heavens it doubtless fell so gently that it would hardly have hurt a baby's face. But now, under its tremendous pressure, small trees were being uprooted and rocks were being rushed out of their places. Why the difference? This water was saying: "This one thing I do." It is only as we are wholeheartedly for Christ that we find our highest personal satisfaction and highest usefulness.

4. Then we ought to decide definitely for Christ, because by refusing to do so we decide against him. There is a fable that a donkey once stood between two delicious bundles of hay. The donkey was hungry. Both bundles offered just the satisfaction he needed. But when he would turn toward the one the other would seem to call to him. Thus he could never make up his mind just which bundle he would eat first. Therefore he hesitated between the two until he starved. His death was not the result of a decision to commit suicide. It was rather the result of his failure to decide to eat.

Even so we miss knowing Jesus Christ through lack of decision. Right now he is offering himself to us. Most of us have declared to him our allegiance in some fashion. But in spite of this some of us are keenly conscious of the fact that our religious lives often have been quite disappointing. We wonder at times if we had not better renounce the whole venture as a failure. What is the way to victory? Make a wholehearted decision. God longs to give you the best, but he cannot without your co-operation. Remember that God's one plan of salvation is for a surrendered heart.

IX

THE TRANSFORMING TOUCH

"Who touched me?"

LUKE 8:45

❦

"WHO touched me?" Simon and his fellow disciples could hardly keep from laughing. What an amazing question for one to ask who was being pushed and elbowed on all sides by an eager and curious crowd. This Master of theirs was unspeakably winsome. He was fascinating beyond all words. They had never seen anyone like him. But what queer things he could sometimes do and say! The idea of asking "Who touched me?" when he was being half crushed by a mob! But they did not laugh at him; they loved him far too well for that. Yet his question did seem as silly to them as it would to us if a friend, while sitting by our side at a Rose Bowl football game, should ask: "Who is seeing the game with us today?"

Naturally Simon simply could not keep from setting his Lord right. Therefore he answered patiently, as to a small child: "Master, the multitude throng thee and press thee, and sayest thou, Who touched me?" What Simon is trying to get across to his Master is that his question is rather ridiculous. He is saying: "Scores of people have touched you, perhaps hundreds. It is therefore impossible for any of us to give a correct answer to your question."

But Jesus was not satisfied with Simon's answer. He was, of course, as keenly aware of the thronging crowd as Simon. But he also knew what this disciple did not know—that one single individual had made contact with him and had thereby been the recipient of his healing power. Therefore, in spite of Simon's explanation, he affirmed: "Somebody hath touched me."

Our Lord found deep joy in being able to make this affirmation. That was the case because he was always eager to give of himself. He rejoiced with joy unspeakable when one needy soul was willing to receive at his hands. It would seem that his greatest heartache while he was here was that he was so eager to give while those about him were so reluctant to receive. Here is a word that is still wet with tears: "Ye will not come to me, that ye might have life." Perhaps the greatest grief of our Lord at this moment is that he longs to do so much for us and we permit him to do so little. Here he was able to say: "Somebody hath touched me." That fact made his heart sing.

But if there was gladness in this word there must have been sorrow as well. There were hundreds, perhaps thousands, in the crowd that thronged about him. Every one of them needed to touch him. Every one of them might have touched him. But only one claimed her privilege. Only one availed herself of her opportunity. The door to a richer and fuller life stood open before all, but only one

94

had the faith to enter. Thus while our Lord rejoiced over the one who touched him, he could not but sorrow over the many who were content merely to throng him.

I

Who was this fortunate soul?

1. She was a woman with a heavy handicap. She had been suffering from a hemorrhage for twelve years. Twelve years is a long time when one is well; it is doubly long when one is fighting with illness. It is longer still when one is making a losing fight. Then hers was a shame-faced disease that made her ceremonially unclean. It seems also to have shut her out from the privilege of wifehood and motherhood. Then too she had consulted various physicians who had relieved her of nothing but her money. Thus to the burden of her illness had been added the additional burden of poverty.

2. She was a woman who clung passionately to life. She was determined not to die until something killed her. I like that. It has always been my conviction that the best way to get ready for the life to come is to love this life and to live it as bravely and faithfully as we can. She therefore did not make a tame surrender to her illness. Having made one effort at recovery she did not lie down in self-pity to enjoy bad health. She refused thus to become a burden both to herself and to others. In spite of all her failures she still possessed a fighting heart. It was this woman, handicapped by illness and many failures, who succeeded in touching Jesus.

II

How did she come to touch him?

1. Mark tells that she heard of Jesus. Naturally. "Faith cometh by hearing." The reason that you touched him in youth's bright morning long ago was because somebody told you about him. That is how I came to touch him. That is how our children will touch him, if at all. We must tell them about him. We must tell them by what we say and especially by what we do. Christianity can be taught. It can also more effectively be caught. This woman heard about Jesus.

Just who was the bearer of this good news we are not told. I imagine that it was some friend, some woman perhaps who had come to know Jesus and who had experienced his healing power. But whoever she was, one day she took time to sit down beside this faded and fading friend and tell her that a new physician had come. She told her further that the fact that she had spent all her money need not deter her from going to him. "He heals without money and without price," she may have declared boldly. "Not only so, but he is in our village today. If I were you, I would give myself a chance by going to him at once."

2. Not only did this woman hear about Jesus, but she believed what she heard. As she listened to her friend faith and hope grew strong in her heart. She said to herself: "I believe that he can heal. I believe that he healed this friend of mine!" Then she passed on to affirm that faith that is of supreme importance: "I believe he can and will heal me. Of course I do not expect healing without any

96

co-operation on my part. But if I do co-operate I can be certain of the results. If I but touch his clothes I shall be healed."

3. Having thus come to believe, she went into action. Faith that is real acts. Faith that does not act is not in reality faith at all. In spite of her weakness, in spite of the fact that some of her friends perhaps looked askance at her and told her how silly she was, she set out on her adventure of faith. In spite of the crowd that got in her way she persisted; she kept telling herself: "If I touch but his clothes I shall be healed."

This woman knew how to talk to herself. That is a fine art. What others say to us is often of vast importance. There are words that can weaken and torture us. There are other words that can strengthen us and that fall upon our wounds like healing balm. But if what others say to us is important, what we say to ourselves is far more important. Tell me what you habitually say to yourself and I will tell you what you are and what increasingly you are becoming.

Who would ever have called the rich farmer a fool had they seen nothing but his shrewd face and his obvious success? But when we hear him talk to himself, when we hear him tell himself that he alone is responsible for his prosperity and that therefore he owes no debt of gratitude either to God or man, then we begin to understand how only one word can adequately describe him and that is the word that God used—"Thou fool."

How did the prodigal son come to turn his steps home? It was because he knew how to talk to himself. When he talked to himself what did he say? Here is what he might have said: "I am the most wretched person in the world. Here I am feeding hogs. But it is not my fault. It is the fault of my father who is as soft-headed as he is soft-hearted. He ought not to have given me my inheritance when I asked him for it. It is the fault of my brother who is as cold as an icicle and hard as a nail. It is the fault of my friends who stood by when I had money and left me when I was broke. It is everybody's fault except mine." Had he talked like that he would have remained in the hogpen until he rotted.

What then did he say? When he came to himself he spoke somewhat after this fashion: "I have made a terrible mess. I came away to have a good time, but I am now literally dying of hunger. Not only so, but I have nobody to blame but myself. It broke my father's heart for me to leave him, but in spite of that I came. Now I am going back and tell him what a mess I have made. I came away in the open light of day; I am going back in the same fashion. I am not going to try to sneak in. I am going to face all the ugly facts and ask for a new chance." Thus talking to himself, he left the hogpen and never stopped going until he felt the hug of his father's arms and the kiss of his father's lips.

This frail woman setting out on her difficult mission might have said some very discouraging things to herself. "How silly you are," she might have said, "to keep trying. Here you are going to a physician who has no diploma from a medical school. Yet you know that the very best physicians have failed to help you." But instead of talking in this fashion she encouraged herself. She told herself that here was one who was different. She told herself: "If I touch but his clothes I shall be healed. Therefore touch I will, regardless of cost." Thus talking to herself, she accomplished her purpose.

III

What was the result?

At once she was healed. Just as an electric light bulb begins to blaze with light the instant it is brought into contact with the dynamo, so this woman received healing power the instant she touched him who is the source of power. Not only was she healed but she was conscious of her healing. She could join her voice with those who through the ages have come to certainty. A once-blind man can leave many questions unanswered without serious hurt if he can affirm: "One thing I know, that, whereas I was blind, now I see." At once this woman knew that she had been healed.

Then it was that Jesus asked: "Who touched me?" Why did he ask that question? It was not because he was seeking information. It was not because he was ignorant regarding this woman. It was rather because he knew that she was ignorant of him. He was not seeking to get her to reveal herself to him, but he was seeking to reveal himself to her. It was her purpose to steal away in silence and not tell the story of her illness any more. But Jesus had something better for her than that. Therefore he asked: "Who touched me?"

Now when the woman saw that the Master knew just

what had taken place, she came, as Mark tells us, "and fell down before him, and told him all the truth." It is well to follow the advice of James and confess our faults one to another and pray one for another. However, I am convinced that there are some confessions that we ought to make to God only. In his presence we can fully "unpack our hearts with words." Without reservation we can tell him all the truth. When this woman had done this Jesus fairly opened the door of a new world to her as he said: "Daughter, thy faith hath made thee whole; go in peace." And we may believe that the Christ who had given her salvation kept her to the end of the journey.

IV

What does this story have to say to us today?

We are separated from this scene by centuries and seas and continents, yet it has a word for us that is as fresh and up to date as our last heartbeat.

1. We, despite the centuries, have much in common with that multitude that thronged Jesus in the long ago. We are confronted with tasks that are too heavy for our strength. We need to be the recipient of his power. Some of us have come with empty lives that we need to hold up to his fullness. Some of us have fears that make us look with painful foreboding for the morrow. Some are lonely and need the comfort of him who has promised to be with us all our days. We have all come with our hungers and thirsts, with our burdens, our fears and our sins, even as these of the long ago.

2. The same Christ who was thronged by the multitude

100

on that distant day still moves among us. This is his own word: "Where two or three are gathered together in my name, there am I in the midst of them." We can count on this fact with absolute conviction. We can count on it, as Livingstone would tell us, because it is the word of a gentleman of the strictest honor.

3. Now since he is here among us we can do one of two things. We can either throng him or we can touch him. If we touch him we must co-operate with him. Doing this, the outcome is sure. We can touch him by our prayers. So the saints have found through the centuries; so some of us have found.

"Speak to Him thou for he hears, and Spirit with Spirit
    can meet—
  Closer is He than breathing, and nearer than hands and
    feet."

Then we can touch him by our obedience. We can touch him by the dedication of our lives to him. This is his own promise: "If any man is willing to do his will, he shall know." This is not theory; it is experience.

"No fable old, nor mythic lore,
    Nor dream of bards and seers;
  No fact stranded on the shore
    Of the oblivious years.

But warm, sweet, tender even yet
    A present help is he;
And faith has still its Olivet,
    And love its Galilee.

The healing of his seamless dress
  Is by our beds of pain;
We touch him in life's throng and press,
  And we are whole again."

Not only can we touch our Lord today, but the contact that we make in the here and now we can keep through all the changing years. Listen to these words: "I am the vine, ye are the branches." That is, we are related to our Lord as the branch is related to the vine. If this is the case our position then is to be one of constant contact. It is only as the branch remains in contact with the vine that it can live. To lose that contact is to wither. So our lives wither when we lose touch with our Lord. But if we live in his fellowship, it becomes true of us what the psalmist sang of God's blessed man in the long ago—"His leaf also shall not wither." To touch the living Christ and continue in his fellowship is surely to become one of God's evergreens.

This is a story of the long ago. But suppose that I had been an eyewitness to the transformation of this woman. All excitement, I tell you what I have just seen. "I was standing right by Jesus," I declare eagerly. "In fact, I was rubbing elbows with him when I saw a frail woman pressing her way through the crowd. My first thought was that she ought to be at home in bed. But I saw that she was bent on some definite purpose. At last she reached out a frail finger and touched the tassel of Jesus' robe. I then rubbed my eyes in utter amazement. I could hardly believe what I saw. At once the roses of health began to bloom on her faded face. Immediately she was healed.

Then I heard the Master say: 'Thy faith hath made thee whole; go in peace.' "

Now were I to speak to you after this fashion you could not leave my story just there. You would have to ask a few questions: "Are you telling me that the woman was healed by a mere touch and that you were fairly rubbing elbows with the Master when this miracle took place? Then what difference did his presence make in you? Were you also transformed?" Should I answer in the negative you would know that I had made no real effort to touch Jesus. I was satisfied merely to throng him. How about you? When he asks, as he is asking now, "Who touched me?" can you give a glad affirmative?

X

THE GREAT DISTURBER

"Suppose ye that I am come to give peace on earth? I tell you, Nay; but rather division."

LUKE 12:51

❧

IT is well for us that Jesus answered this question. Personally I should never have given the reply that he did. On the contrary, I should have answered with a most emphatic affirmative. In so doing I should have had solid scriptural backing. That Jesus came to bring peace is affirmed by his very name. He is the Prince of Peace. This is further declared by the song that the angels sang at his birth, a song of peace and good will. Jesus himself affirmed it further during his ministry by saying to more than one tempest-tossed soul: "Go in peace." He affirmed it finally by the legacy that he left us when he went away: "Peace I leave with you, my peace I give unto you. . . . Let not your heart be troubled, neither let it be afraid."

But in spite of my confident affirmation that Jesus has come to bring peace, he answers his own question by an emphatic denial. "Suppose ye that I am come to give peace on earth? . . . Nay; but rather division." Instead of "division" Matthew substitutes the word "sword." This makes his answer even more shocking if possible. Here then is the Prince of Peace declaring that he has not come to bring peace, but a sword. In other words, this Prince of Peace has come as a disturber, a creator of discord. Surely this is a paradox that needs some explaining.

I

When Jesus declared that he is a disturber, a creator of division, he was speaking sober truth. In fact, he was and is the most disturbing personality that ever walked this earth. When he was on trial for his life much of the testimony offered against him was utterly false. But there was at least one charge that his accusers brought that was true. Had his prosecutors been so minded they could have called a thousand witnesses to prove it. That charge was this: "He stirreth up the people." Indeed he did. Wherever he went sedate and quiet villages came to seethe with turmoil and confusion. In fact, his whole nation felt the impact of his personality. It became as fretted and restless as a sea whipped by a storm.

One day, for instance, Jesus attended church in his home town. It was a Sabbath, and the atmosphere, I dare say, was pervaded by the serenity and calm of that holy day. When the congregation had assembled Jesus himself read the lesson of the day. It was that beautiful passage from Isaiah which begins like this: "The Spirit of the Lord is upon me, because he hath anointed me to preach." Then, as he proceeded with his sermon, his hearers were spellbound. They could not but wonder at the gracious words that fell from his lips. It seemed as if the service was destined to be one of the high spots in their lives.

But not only did Jesus have gracious words for his fellow worshipers, but he even had something gracious to say about certain rank outsiders. "There were many lepers in Israel during the days of Elisha the prophet," he declared in effect, "but not one of them had faith to be healed. The only man possessed of such faith was a foreinger named Naaman. There were many widows in Israel when Elijah had a price on his head and was hunting for a boarding place. But the only widow who dared give him shelter was a pagan of the land from which Jezebel came." At this the service was thrown into confusion. The Sabbath calm was shattered by the protests of angry men. A mob was formed, and those present could account for the escape of Jesus only by saying that it was a miracle.

On another day Jesus came to a bit of countryside near the village of Gadera. This too was in the main a quiet place. "Along the cool sequester'd vale of life" the native farmers and swineherds "kept the noiseless tenor of their way." True, there was a certain lunatic in the neighborhood who created a disturbance now and then. But he lived in the cemetery and gave only occasional trouble.

But with the coming of Jesus there was a real disturbance. For no sooner had he come upon the scene than he cured this lunatic. When therefore the neighbors saw this once-madman seated at the feet of Jesus, clothed and in his right mind, they were naturally excited. But far more exciting and disturbing was the fact that, seemingly in the process of working the cure, Jesus had had to sacrifice a whole herd of hogs. "What," they ask in terror, "is to be done with a man who thinks more of a bit of human wreckage than of a herd of good hogs?" They felt that something must be done and that at once. So not daring to try to drive out so powerful a personality, they sent a committee tactfully to request Jesus to depart out of their coasts. The man who puts human values first is always a disturber.

Then Jesus disturbed men individually. I dare say there was no man in his community more honored and respected than the rich young ruler. He possessed so much worthwhile treasure. He had youth, wealth, and position. He was earnestly religious. He was doubtless fairly contented with himself and his lot. Then rumors about Jesus began to blow his way. When he heard what this young rabbi was doing, how unselfishly he was using his life, he was disturbed. His inward conflict reached a climax one day when he heard that Jesus was passing along the highway. So disturbed was he that, patrician though he was, he ran to kneel at the feet of this peasant to ask how to find life. Sad to say, the price was higher than he was willing to pay. But though he went away he did not go joyfully. He rather went with an ache in his heart and a sob in his throat. Thus did Jesus rob him of the bit of false peace that he might have possessed.

That great revolutionary who died beside Jesus was no ordinary criminal. He was an ardent patriot who had dedicated his life to the service of his counquered country. Unable to organize armies and fight in the open, he had staged one raid after another in which there had, no doubt, been considerable bloodletting. But he had become a revolutionary with his eyes wide open to its cost. So when he had been captured and brought to justice his one regret was that he had not inflicted greater injury upon the enemy. Therefore he walked bravely toward Calvary under the weight of his wooden cross. Like a man he had fought, and like a man he was determined to die.

But something happened that turned what tranquility he had into utter turmoil. Against the white background of the man on the central cross he saw himself. Therefore, though he was suffering the tortures of hell, he declared that he was suffering justly. In fact, so great was his inner agony that the agony of his tortured body was forgotten. His pain was not in being where he was, but in being what he was. Therefore he turned to his dying companion with this prayer: "Lord, remember me when thou comest into thy kingdom."

Thus Jesus divided men within themselves. Thus he divided man from man. Some who touched him loved him with a love that nothing could kill. Others hated him with a hatred that nailed him to a cross. These two groups, therefore, were separated from each other by distances wider than the spaces between the stars. Jesus was and is the great disturber. He has come to bring division.

II

Why is this the case?

1. Jesus disturbs us by being what he is. When I was a small boy my utter aversion to all schoolwork made me

108

the despair of my family. In sober truth, I never intended to learn to read. I did not even want to learn. There were so many other things that seemed more worth-while. But one day there came a little girl, some two years younger than myself, to spend the summer in our home. I showed her my prowess with the horses and the cattle. I was a good rider and her admiration thrilled my boyish soul. But I soon saw that she was far different from me. She was a great reader. She made me feel for the first time that my ignorance was an ugly and shameful thing. So much was this the case that I said to myself: "Someday I am going to know as much as she." And life for me at that time took on a new departure.

Years ago each worker in the Hugh Price Hughes Mission in London was accustomed to wear a white carnation. One day one of these workers sat talking to a young woman who was an outcast. Suddenly this young woman burst into tears. The worker was puzzled because she was not discussing anything to stir her emotions. When she sought to know the cause of her tears, the young woman touched the white flower and said: "I am not like that. I wish I were white and clean like that flower." Thus when we face Jesus we are forced to say: "I am not like that." He disturbs us by being what he is.

2. He disturbs us through natural law. This world is built on a basis of righteousness. When we do wrong we suffer. That suffering is not our foe; it is our friend. If you have a diseased appendix that disease announces itself in the convincing words of pain. That pain may be very unwelcome, yet it is the red flag that nature waves in

109

your face to tell you that something is wrong. If this disease were to fail to announce itself you might die without ever knowing what was the matter.

Now there are laws of spiritual health just as there are laws of physical health. When I sin against my body I suffer. When I sin against my better self I suffer too. Take hate, for instance. Hate may cause me to do injury to one against whom I hold a grudge. But if I am too civilized to try to injure my enemy, that hate will still tear my life to bits and make it a veritable hell. By making me sick spiritually it will often make me sick physically as well. I knew a woman who died not long ago, and it is my honest conviction that she died largely of hate.

Then we have social, national, even world-wide agonies. These at times express themselves in costly conflicts between capital and labor. They express themselves, though at rarer intervals I am happy to say, in terms of mob violence. They express themselves in terms of wars that all but wreck the world. All these tragic pains are the outward eruptions of an inward rottenness. They are voices calling to us, in language that we cannot wholly ignore, to set the house of life in order.

Today, for instance, there is widespread hunger for peace. It is not the result, I am sorry to say, of a new sense of brotherhood. I fear that we do not love each other any better than did our fathers. But we are driven to seek a warless world because of what we have suffered. Thus our Lord disturbs us by the painful consequences of our sins.

3. Then Jesus disturbs us of set purpose. There is a

word in Genesis that says: "My spirit shall not always strive with man." But God does strive with us here and now with patient persistence. Constantly he is saying: "Behold, I stand at the door, and knock." He will never permit any of us to sleep our way into disaster without doing his best to rouse us into wakefulness. Our dissatisfaction with ourselves, our longing to be better, our passion to be of service, all these are but the disturbing voices of our Lord calling us to our best possibilities.

III

Now what is the purpose of our Lord in thus disturbing us?

He is robbing us of our false peace in order to give us one that is real. For we may be sure after all that Jesus has come to bring peace on earth. But he can give us this peace only through our co-operation. This is the case because peace is a consequence. It is an effect rather than a cause. To find peace therefore we must be willing to meet the conditions of peace. We must be willing to give up whatever is antagonistic to peace. Unless we meet these conditions not even God himself can give us peace.

When I was a barefoot boy I would often have a stone bruise. This was a painful experience and I eagerly sought for peace. I would try one poultice after another. But all in vain. The only remedy that worked was the lance. The corruption caused by the bruise had to be let out. Even so our Lord declares that there are ills that demand spiritual surgery: "If thy right eye offend thee, pluck it out. . . . If thy right hand offend thee, cut it off."

111

That is, we must be willing to get rid of that which disturbs our peace, even though it prove as painful as the cutting off of the right hand or the plucking out of the right eye.

When the prophet said "There is no peace . . . to the wicked," he was not making a threat, but stating a fact. Paul was speaking to the same purpose when he said: "The kingdom of God is not eating and drinking, but righteousness and peace and joy in the Holy Spirit." (A.S.V.) We do not find peace merely by having plenty to eat and plenty to drink. Before there can be any real peace there must be righteousness. This means rightness—rightness with God, rightness within, rightness between man and man. Any temple of peace that we seek to build upon a foundation of unrighteousness and injustice will fall into ruins however full of promise it may seem.

How then shall we find peace? It is first of all an individual matter. We shall find it as we give ourselves in wholehearted obedience to the Prince of Peace.

Some years ago a returned missionary told this story. "As I was coming down from the Himalaya Mountains I saw a man in the distance climbing to meet me. When we drew closer together I heard the clank of chains. Closer still I could see that the man had a huge chain about his neck that had almost worn the flesh from his chest. I could not pass him by without a question, so I asked him to tell me his story. He then told me that a few years before he had gone to his priest in search of peace. This priest had told him to perform certain extremely hard penances. He had obeyed only to be disappointed. At last the priest had put

112

that heavy chain about his neck and had told him to climb to the summit of the mountain up which he was then toiling.

"When I had heard this story," the missionary continued, "I reached up and took the chain from his neck and asked him to sit down beside me. Then I told him about the Prince of Peace. I told him that peace was a gift of Jesus Christ, that he could receive it as a gift by the giving of himself. At once the light of understanding came into his eyes and the glory of God broke over his face. The last I saw of him he was going back to tell those of his native village about the Prince of Peace."

Yes, Jesus has come to bring peace on earth, peace to your heart and mine, and peace throughout the world. But he can give that peace only when we give our all to him.

XI

SIN AND SUFFERING

*"Suppose ye that these Galileans were sin-
ners above all the Galileans, because they
suffered such things?"*

LUKE 13:2

❧

CERTAIN individuals had just rushed into the presence of Jesus bearing tragic tidings. I have an idea
that these messengers were Judeans. If so they looked
askance at these suffering Galileans as crude folks from
the sticks. Therefore it was with more elation than tears
that they told the Master of how these Galileans had come
to worship, but had ended by having their own blood
mingled with the blood of the beasts that they were offering in sacrifice. What terrible sinners they must have been!
That is what they meant to imply as they told their heavy
news.

But Jesus did not agree with them. Instead he told them
frankly that this tragedy did not indicate that these slaughtered saints were worse than their fellows. If you and I
are in an automobile accident and you are killed and I

escape, that does not argue that you were wicked while I am good. Instead of agreeing with these men Jesus affirmed that they themselves were just as real sinners as those who had suffered. He declared further that unless they should repent they too would perish. It is evident as we read this story that these ancient bearers of evil tidings were possessed of certain convictions that were a strange mixture of truth and error, or of truth and half-truth.

I

There was one conviction that they held that is 100 per cent true. They were firm in the faith that sin always results in suffering. In their own scriptures they read this emphatic word: "Be sure your sin will find you out." This they steadfastly believed; this we should do well to believe. It was true in the long ago; it is true today. It was true in a primitive society; it is true in our scientific age. Every man who sins turns loose a nemesis upon his tracks that he can no more escape than he can escape his own shadow. "Be sure your sin will find you out." Your friends, your loved ones may never find you out. The officers of the law may fail, but your sin, never.

This is the case not because God is angry at the sinner. It is rather the case because we live in a law-abiding world. We live in a world where this law is forever true: "Whatsoever a man soweth, that shall he also reap." This is a solemn word of warning that we have chiefly used to cudgel sinners into being obedient. But it is more than a warning—it is a radiant promise. It tells us that we have it in our power to determine beyond a peradventure the quality of harvest we are going to reap tonight, tomorrow night, to the end of life, and to the end of eternity. That is something for which to be devoutly grateful.

In one of *McGuffey's Readers* there is the story of a man who barked his shins against this law of sowing and reaping until he cried out in bitterness: "I wish I were in a world of chance." Having thus wished, the author tells us that he went to sleep to awake in a world where law had ceased to reign. Suddenly he got the toothache. He sought relief by undertaking to make a pot of hot coffee. But when he took this supposedly hot coffee into his mouth he found it to be full of ice. "What does this mean?" he asked, as he spat it out in indignation. "It doesn't mean anything," came the reply. "We put the coffee on the fire. Sometimes the fire boils it and sometimes it freezes it. But it is your kind of world." Naturally, he longed to get back into his ordered world. That is the only kind of world in which life is livable.

But whether we appreciate the fact that ours is an ordered world or whether we resent it, the law of sowing and reaping still operates. Years ago when I was a pastor in Houston a good woman gave her son a secondhand automobile. This young man, who was just getting well into his teens, enjoyed driving his car at high speed around curves in order to hear the tires screak. One morning as he was indulging in this pastime his car skidded and ran into a telephone pole. He was thrown through the windshield against the pole and an ambulance came and hurried him to the hospital. They phoned for the minister and when I reached the hospital his mother was almost frantic. She

116

grasped my hands in both of hers and exclaimed: "Why should this happen to me?"

Her question silenced me for an instant, then I answered: "It did not happen to you, it happened to him."

"But why did God let it happen," she continued.

"Hold on," I replied, "don't blame God for permitting this accident. If our Lord were to snatch a telephone pole from in front of your son when he was driving recklessly, he might set one in front of me when I was driving carefully. In that case none of us could drive intelligently. All I am arguing is that every man must hit his own telephone pole."

So must every group; so must every nation. If the law of gravity operates for me when I walk on the ground and thus keeps me from flying out into space, I cannot expect it to go into reverse when I step out a tenth-story window.

Of course there was a sense in which this accident did happen to the mother. She suffered in the suffering of her son because she was bound up in the bundle of life with him. The vast majority of the suffering that we experience in this world, I am sure, comes from our own individual and collective wrong choices. But even when we are not personally guilty we often suffer because we are members one of another. Here, for instance, is a horrible sentence. On the surface it sounds positively devilish: "Visiting the iniquity of the fathers upon the children unto the third and fourth generation."

"How unjust!" I might exclaim. "Why should a guilty father have the power to visit his guilt upon me? How unfair that I should be handicapped by the loose and lustful life of one in whose sin I had no share." But that is the price I pay for the capacity of being helped by a father and grandfather who lived clean and Christlike lives. If their sins are visited upon me, so also are their faith and goodness and Christlikeness. If by wrong living I have power to hurt my children, by right living I also have power to reach a hand even across the chasm of death to steady them and give them an upward lift.

Just as we are bound in a bundle of life with our children, so are we with our fellows everywhere. We are bound in a bundle of life with the nations. Not long ago I read a fiery speech that urged that we withhold our help from Europe and the rest of the world and spend our money making ourselves strong. In other words, we are to save ourselves as did the priest and the Levite, by passing by on the other side. But that is salvation that ends in damnation. This is the case simply because we are part of the world. We belong to the family of nations. We are bound even more closely with the Negroes who live among us. Therefore if one member suffers all members suffer with him.

Some months ago while fishing I got some poison ivy on my left ankle. Now if you have ever had anything to do with such poison you know that it can be very diverting. If any of you find difficulty in staying awake while your minister preaches, I can assure you that you will have no trouble at all if you manage to contract poison ivy. When I realized what had happened I remembered how I used to treat the ailment when I was a boy. I was accus-

118

tomed to cure it by applications of carbolic acid. So I hurried to the drugstore and obtained a small bottle of the remedy.

But there was one item that I forgot. As a boy I used to dilute the acid. Instead, this time I took mine straight. I rubbed it on and rubbed it in. Then I got action. When the acid had eaten down close to the bone my whole body had an insurrection. My hand said: "I will have nothing to do with it. I am going to see to it that that offending member keeps its place." My head vowed that it would have nothing to do with it, saying: "That ankle is now burned black and red." But though every member of my body was an isolationist, when we went to bed that evening we all stayed awake together. Here then is a conviction held by the ancient Jews that is certainly true. Sin always eventuates in suffering. The sinner suffers, also those bound in a bundle of life with him.

II

But along with this certainty that is true everywhere and in every age there were other convictions that were mixtures of truth and of error.

1. Believing that sin always results in suffering, they affirmed with equal conviction that righteousness always escapes. They therefore would have said "Amen" to that mistranslated word of the first psalm that, speaking of God's blessed man, says, "Whatsoever he doeth shall prosper." Now the psalmist did not really say that, as we shall see later. But it was their faith that while the wicked man always went to the wall, the good man always won

119

the prize. He prospered physically and financially as well as spiritually.

Now there is a measure of truth in this. Certainly it is a fact, other things being equal, that the good man stands a better chance of physical health than the evil man. He also stands a better chance to prosper financially. A leading civic club has this as its motto: "He profits most who serves the best." Men in business have discovered that honesty and fair dealing are profitable. Thus a decent clean-living man has a far better chance at worldly success than his opposite.

But while this is true it does not mean that goodness is an infallible road to success. It might be very impressive to see all the rascals go bankrupt and all the saints get rich, but that is not the way life works. What therefore the psalmist really said is this: "In whatsoever he doeth he shall prosper." His bank may fail, his business may go to the wall, his physical strength may give way to weakness, but God's blessed man himself will prosper in spite of it all. The belief therefore that the righteous always succeeds is only a half-truth.

2. Convinced that sin always results in suffering, they believed that wherever any man suffered he suffered as a result of his own sin. Of course this is often the case. All of us have known those who have suffered the pangs of hell in their own souls and in their own bodies who had no one to blame for that suffering but themselves. Years ago I had a brilliant friend who threw away priceless possessions of ability to plunge into a mad orgy of dissipation. He held himself back from nothing that he thought

would give him a thrill. By-and-by, he became a sober clean-living man. He told his own story in this fashion. "I have given up my wild and foolish ways. This I have done not because I have become a Christian, at least I have not become a Christian yet. But I changed my way of living because I got tired of suffering." Many a man who has gaily sowed to the flesh is today reaping his harvest with bitter anguish and tears.

But while this is true it does not mean that all who suffer are paying the penalty for their own sin. When Job had lost his wealth, when he had lost his loved ones, when pain had come to walk with fireshod feet along every nerve of his body, three friends came to comfort him but remained to torture him. They had a very easy reading of the problem of his pain. They said that he was suffering as a result of his own sin. To their way of thinking it could not be otherwise. Therefore they asked him this quenching question: "Who ever perished being innocent?" The answer to that is "Multitudes." Jesus Christ himself was such a sufferer. If there are those who suffer because they are so evil there are also those who suffer because they are so good. Therefore we cannot say that everyone who suffers is paying the penalty for his own sin.

3. Being sure that sin always results in suffering, they reached the erroneous conclusion that because they themselves were not suffering they therefore had not sinned. This does not necessarily mean that they were claiming absolute perfection, but they were profoundly sure that they had not sinned so greatly as these miserable creatures

121

whom Pilate had slaughtered. This false conviction did not make them better. It made them far worse.

This was the case in the first place because it ministered to their pride and self-righteousness. They did not look at these poor Galileans and say: "There go we except for the grace of God." They rather said: "You ought to have been good like us then you would not have suffered." Therefore instead of looking upon those sufferers with compassion and humility they regarded them with prideful contempt.

A second result of their freedom from suffering was the conviction that even though they might have sinned in some respectable fashion they were getting away with their sin. They were still sure of course that men reap as they sow. That is, they were sure that the ordinary run of the mill do that. But such was not quite true for themselves. They were shrewd enough to manipulate the laws of nature and to gather grapes of thorns and figs of thistles. Thus they had not only become self-righteous and contemptuous in the presence of the suffering of others, but they had become morally color-blind. They had come to believe that for themselves a crooked line might at times be the shortest distance between two points. That was the very climax of tragedy. This is the case because sin is never so tragic as when it seems to triumph. It is never so deadly as when it seems to give life. It always brings disaster, but it is never quite so disastrous as when we seem to get by with it.

III

What did our Lord have to say to these men? He called them to repentance. This he did because they were sinners just as were those whom Pilate had slaughtered. They were sinners just as we are. There is no difference, said Paul, "for all have sinned." By this he does not mean that we have all sinned equally. There were two thorn trees that grew side by side on my father's farm. One of these had very few thorns while the other had thousands. But the one that was almost free of thorns could not for that reason say to its fellow: "You are a thorn tree, but I am a weeping willow." They were both thorn trees still. These needed to repent because they were sinners, even as you and I.

Now Jesus seems to regard repentance as the supreme antidote to suffering. What is it to repent? It is something more than being convinced that you are a sinner. It is something more than being sorry for sin. I am thinking of a man who used to turn from his slimy ways with his throat choked with sobs and his face wet with tears. Repentance is being so sorry for sin that we turn from it to God. The prodigal repented when he left the swinepen and kept going until he found the shelter of his father's arms. Repentance is the supreme antidote against suffering for two reasons.

First, repentance saves us from suffering because it prevents our wrong choices. We do not by repentance escape in the here and now the consequences of our wrongdoing. We must repent before we sin if we are to save

123

ourselves and others from the suffering that always follows in the wake of wrongdoing. After Esau had sold his birthright his tears over his tragic folly were vain tears, not because God refused to forgive, since God did forgive him fully and freely. But they were vain because his belated repentance could not put back into his hands the opportunities that he had thrown away in youth's bright morning long ago. If therefore you would spare yourself and others the penalty of pain, repent before you sin.

2. Then repentance, because it brings us within the will of God, helps to solve the problem of pain. This is the case because "All things work together for good to them that love God." If we co-operate with God by so loving him as to obey him, we make it possible for him to change all our losses into gains. As nature sometimes takes the wound of an oyster and changes it into a pearl, even so God can take our wounds, whatever their cause, and make them into jewels of priceless worth. Meet your suffering within his will and you too will be able to say: "We know that all things work together for good to them that love God."

XII

PERSISTENT PRAYER

"Shall not God?"

LUKE 18:7

❦

"SHALL not God?" Through the story of which this question is a part Jesus is undertaking to teach us the importance and the reasonableness of a habit of prayer. He realized quite as well as we how easy it is for one to become discouraged in an effort to pray. He knows how prone we are to turn aside from this task that might be so rewarding to give ourselves to lesser tasks that seem to bring greater results. Knowing the tragedy of such failure he fairly taxes his vast abilities in an effort to teach us that we ought always to pray and not to faint.

I

Jesus taught us to pray by what he said about prayer.

His assertions regarding the privileges and possibilities of prayer often seem to our dim faith extravagant. He tells us, for instance, that prayer is not the privilege of the few but of the many. It is not simply for those who have climbed far up the hill toward God, but it is for ordinary plodders like ourselves. He asserts that everyone that asketh, receiveth; that he that seeketh, findeth; and that to him that knocketh, it shall be opened. The victories of prayer may be won by even the weakest.

Even so, failure may come to the strongest without it. One day Jesus came upon his disciples to find them hot and flustered. They had just made a terrible failure and were therefore filled with shame and confusion. A father had brought to them his afflicted lad. They had undertaken to cure him. But all their efforts had proved futile. They had succeeded only in winning the ridicule of the scoffers and in weakening the faith of this father who had come with such high confidence. But when Jesus came on the scene defeat was changed into victory. When therefore these disciples were alone with their Master they asked him this sane question: "Why could not we cast him out?"

What answer did our Lord give? He did not attribute their failure to their indifference. They were interested both in this father and in his son. Neither did he tell them that they had failed because of a lack of effort. They had done their serious and earnest best. No more did he tell them that their failure was due to the fact that they had undertaken a task that was too big for them, even when assisted by divine strength. He rather declared that they had failed in their efforts to help because they had failed to pray. If we refuse to pray, no amount of effort will atone for that failure when we go forth to battle.

But if what Jesus said about prayer was so impressive what he did about it was more impressive still. It was not after a sermon on prayer that the disciples came saying: "Lord, teach us to pray," but it was after they had seen the Master on his knees. As they watched him at prayer they said: "Here is something real. Here is something far bigger and finer than we have ever done. Here is something that is supremely worth-while. We must learn the secret." Not only did they feel the reality and the worth of prayer when they saw the Master upon his knees, but they were heartened to believe that such praying was in some measure possible for themselves. Therefore they came with this wise prayer: "Lord, teach us to pray."

Our Lord is teaching us still. What place did he give to prayer in his own busy and triumphant life? The answer is that he gave prayer first place. Prayer was central in the life of Jesus. With us prayer is sometimes a preparation for the battle, but with Jesus prayer, in a very genuine sense, was the battle. That is, having prayed he went as an honor student might go to receive a medal or as a victor might go to receive the spoils of his conquest.

To be convinced of this it is only necessary to turn again to the Gospels. Here we see Jesus when he was obviously putting forth the utmost of his energy. Here we see him engaged in a conflict so strenuous that his sweat was as great drops of blood falling down to the ground. But there are other times when he walks with a serenity and poise that leave us amazed and wistful to this hour. When, let me ask you, were his seasons of conflict and of struggle, when his seasons of serenity and poise? Always his times of conflict were his prayer periods. If we are to judge by the New Testament the only work that ever really taxed the strength of Jesus was the work of prayer. Having prayed, I repeat, he went forth from the place of prayer as a victor to receive the spoils of his conquest.

Take Jesus' works of wonder, for instance. How easily they were performed! There was no sweat, no agony. When, for instance, a blind beggar asked to be led out of darkness into light, all Jesus had to do was to say: "Receive thy sight." When he stood by the grave of Lazarus there was no struggle, no desperate wringing of hands, only a simple prayer of thanksgiving: "Father, I thank thee that thou hast heard me." Then he called his friend from death to life. It all seems so easy.

Just as there was no agony, no bloody sweat in the doing of his works of wonder, no more was there in his dealing with the shrewd and hostile adversaries that dogged his steps toward the end of his ministry. These men would have given their very lives to have entrapped Jesus into uttering some unguarded word. They set their traps with consummate cunning. Yet he brushed these traps aside like so many cobwebs. Had a stenographer taken down his every word I daresay he would not have had to change his manuscript in the least. Having done well the work of prayer all else seemed to be easy.

It was so even to the end. Had I witnessed the struggle of Jesus in Gethsemane as "he offered up prayers and supplications with strong crying and tears," I should have been afraid for the future. I should have thought: "If he is so broken up now, how utterly will he go to pieces when he meets death eye to eye! Why does he not face the ordeal with the calm confidence of his three sleeping friends?" But when the final test came it was the three friends who went to pieces. It was before the kingly majesty of the man who had prayed that the soldiers staggered back and fell to the ground. Thus Jesus teaches us to pray both by what he said and by what he did.

II

What are some of the rewards of prayer?

1. The first and all-inclusive reward of prayer is that it lets God into our lives. To pray is to open the door to the Christ who is always knocking and waiting for us to invite him to enter. The eternal God becomes real to the one who truly prays. This, I repeat, is the all-inclusive good. There is absolutely nothing so much needed by all of us in these difficult days as a new sense of God. We can find this sense of God individually and as a group by prayer. When we enter a church where men and women pray we are constantly constrained to say: "Surely the Lord is in this place."

This, I repeat, is the all-inclusive blessing of prayer. If you are able to say with the psalmist: "I sought the Lord, and he heard me," if you have ever had an answer to prayer, the biggest thrill of that answer was not the gift that was put into your hands and into your heart. It was rather the new consciousness of God that came to you through that answer. This is the case because no gift can possibly be so great as the giver himself. The richest reward of prayer is a new awareness of the eternal God.

2. Because prayer brings a sense of God it also brings new courage and new power. That is only natural. How-

ever great our danger may be, however grim our foes, if God is real to us we can face them with steady eyes and quiet hearts. "I have set the Lord always before me: because he is at my right hand, I shall not be moved."

When the prophet said: "They that wait upon the Lord shall renew their strength," he was speaking out of his own experience as well as that of countless others. Some of you, I am sure, have found yourselves girded with a strength in the face of difficulty that was a thrill to your soul. Stanley declared that having found Livingstone in Africa, and then having found Livingstone's God, he came to be possessed of a stamina and a courage that his nonpraying companions did not possess. Beyond all doubt, prayer makes it possible for God to do in us and for us and through us what he simply cannot do if we fail to pray.

If you are finding yourself inadequate to the demands that life makes upon you, try prayer. What a fascinating story is that of the triumph of Daniel! When the politicians had secured the king's signature to a law that no man should pray to anybody for the next thirty days but the king himself, they were sure they had Daniel where they wanted him. But it so happened that Daniel was a praying man. Therefore when he knew that his death warrant had been signed he went up into his room and opened his window toward Jerusalem and prayed as he had done "aforetime." That is, prayer had been a habit of his life. That habit stood him in such good stead that he was able to see this trying hour through with honor. Babylon has been a ruin for long centuries. The one thing left standing in it is the character of this man who knew how to pray. Prayer brings power.

3. Prayer is a means of helping others. This was the faith of Jesus. When he foresaw the sifting of Simon he prayed for him. On the night before he went away he prayed with and for his disciples. He also prayed for you and me on that fateful night. This he did when he made request not only for his present disciples, but for all who should believe on him through their word. Not only did Jesus pray for us when he walked among us, but he prays for us still. If we may believe our own Scriptures, prayer is one of the tasks that engages our glorified Christ to this hour. He is even now making intercession for us. Surely he believed in the efficacy of prayer for others.

Paul, who to a superlative degree shared the mind of Christ, shared his faith in prayer. He was constantly remembering his own converts, his friends—all men—in prayer. He was as constantly asking for the prayers of others. He never wrote but one letter, and that to the back-slidden church of Galatia, without asking for the prayers of those backward and faulty believers. He was sure that the very weakest of them could so pray as to anoint his apostolic lips with grace and power.

Since prayer is a means of helping others it is more than a privilege, it is a solemn duty. "God forbid that I should sin against the Lord in ceasing to pray for you." If you find that the services in your church are wanting in warmth and power, try prayer. Pray for your minister that he may be able to bring to you and others a sense of God. Pray for your choir. Pray for the officers and teachers in your church school. It is impossible to have a futile church or a futile service where members of the congregation really pray.

Since we can help by praying we ought to pray. Withholding prayer is a sin. The priest and the Levite who passed by on the other side have sat in the prisoner's dock along with the brigands for long centuries. But if we can pass by on the other side by failing to help by our gifts and by our efforts to bind another's wounds, we can also pass by on the other side by our failure to pray. "Ye also helping together by prayer," writes Paul. Therefore because we can help by prayer it is our duty to help. Withheld prayer is a sin.

Not only can we help by prayer, but there come times when it is the only way we can help. We can give of our money to the cause of missions if we have it. But even if we are too poor to give even a few pennies we can help by prayer. There come desperate hours in the life of those we love when we can help them in no other way. I have had occasion to think of what a terrible thing it would be to be unable to pray when there was nothing else that could be done for the one you love most dearly. There are times when it is the only means. Therefore let your voice rise like a fountain day and night both for yourself and for those who call you friend.

III

How then are we to pray? I am going to offer three suggestions:

1. If prayer is to accomplish its purpose we must pray

earnestly. God cannot give his best to the listless and the halfhearted. It is the earnest, energized prayer that is a mighty force. When John Knox prayed, "Give me Scotland or I die," God gave him Scotland because he could trust his people in the hands of one who was thus desperately in earnest to bring them spiritual health.

If therefore we are to find the best in prayer we must be in earnest about it. God cannot do much for us until we get to the end of ourselves. It is only when the heavy hands of a great need grip our shoulders and crush us to our knees that we really pray. Nothing worth-while is accomplished by the prayers of the halfhearted. Therefore if you would pray effectively you must be in earnest.

2. Pray expectantly. Remember that prayer is not a weird, strange experience. It is the very climax of sanity and common sense. Jesus reminds us that prayer is something with which we have to do in our relations with each other every day that we live. For instance, parents hear and answer prayer. "If a son shall ask bread of any of you that is a father, will he give him a stone?" No good father would be so heartless as to give his boy a stone on which to break his teeth when the boy needed bread. If we then with our imperfections answer the prayers of our children, how much more will God, the perfect father, "give good things to them that ask him."

The reasonableness and sanity of prayer is seen in the relation of friend with friend. When a certain villager was surprised at midnight by an unexpected guest, he was embarrassed by the fact that he had no bread to set before him. So what? He went out to knock on the door of the

133

house of a friend. This friend was in bed. It would seem that he had had trouble with the children and was afraid that this troublesome seeker after bread would disturb them. But in spite of all difficulties he got up and gave his friend as much as he needed.

As a climax Jesus declared that not only do fathers and friends answer prayer, but even heartless scoundrels. In proof of this he told the story of a judge with no regard for either God or man. Yet a widow, the very embodiment of helplessness, so prayed as to win a favorable answer from this cruel and crooked man. This she did in spite of the fact that he cared nothing for her nor for the rightness of her cause. He only hated being bothered. If such a judge will answer prayer, how confident we may be when we pray to a God who is at once a just judge, a loving friend, and a perfect father.

3. Finally, we must pray persistently. We are not to persist in order to make God hear us. We are to persist because we are sure that he will hear us. Once I went to a wedding rehearsal. The bride was thirty minutes late. I confess that I grew a bit restless, but the groom waited with calm confidence. I felt like saying: "Maybe she is not coming. Let us all give over and go home." But the groom was sure that she would come, therefore he waited. But his waiting was not in order to make her come; it was rather because he was sure that she would come. "And shall not God avenge his own elect, which cry day and night unto him, though he bear long with them? I tell you that he will avenge them speedily." Because this is true we ought always to pray and not to faint.

134

XIII

THE GREAT NECESSITY

"Ought not Christ to have suffered these things, and to enter into his glory?"

LUKE 24:26

❧

IT was the first Easter Sunday. Jesus, our risen Lord, was abroad in his springtime world. In the richness of his love and mercy he has drawn near and entered into conversation with two of his grief-stricken friends who were on their way home from his funeral. Though the hearts of these two desolate friends burned within them as he talked with them by the way and opened to them the scriptures, they did not recognize them. This was the case, I dare say, partly because they were not expecting to see him, but more because their eyes were so fixed upon a cross on a skull-shaped hill and upon a tomb in Joseph's garden that they were blind to all else.

But in spite of their failure to recognize him their bleak winter was so thawed by his presence that they soon found themselves opening their hearts to him. Feeling that he would understand, they told him of their young and fearless prophet. They told of the daring hopes they had once cherished because of him. So daring had been these hopes that they had seen in this martyred prophet their own redeemer and the redeemer of Israel. But now that he was dead all hope had died with him; for what could a crucified Christ do for the redemption of a lost world?

Then it was that with great tenderness, and yet with pained disappointment, our Lord answered: "O fools, and slow of heart to believe all that the prophets have spoken: ought not Christ to have suffered these things, and to enter into his glory?" Of course "ought" is not used here in the sense that his suffering was deserved. This modern translation best brings out the meaning: "Was it not necessary that the Christ should suffer these things?" It is therefore evident from this passage that Jesus looked upon his cross not as a tragic misfortune, but as a necessity.

I

This was certainly the case as Jesus looked at the cross in prospect. It is evident to every candid reader of the Gospels that the cross did not take Jesus by surprise. Before he was called upon thus to suffer he had come to look upon that suffering as a necessity. As to the exact date when Jesus began thus to foresee the cross, we may differ. But as to the fact there can be no difference for those who take the New Testament seriously. Jesus himself spoke of his coming tragic death again and again and always he regarded it as a necessity.

When, for instance, he went for a retreat with his

disciples to Caesarea Philippi, he asked these friends as to the impression he had made upon them. When Simon had made his great confession Jesus concluded that they were far enough forward to face the cross. "From that time forth began Jesus to shew unto his disciples, how that he must go unto Jerusalem, and suffer many things of the elders and chief priests and scribes, and be killed, and be raised again the third day."

Later on, when the cross had come so near that he was being put under arrest, his friends were at once heart-broken and bewildered. They could not see how one so vital, one so like God, could allow himself to be done to death. Simon even struck a futile blow with his sword. But the Master spoke home to his bewilderment and despair with these words: "Thinkest thou that I cannot now pray to my Father, and he shall presently give me more than twelve legions of angels? But how then shall the Scriptures be fulfilled, that thus it must be?" It is as if the Master were saying: "I could escape, but only by failing to carry out the full purpose of God for my life."

Then came that lonely struggle in Gethsemane. Here it seems that for a moment Jesus hoped that there might be some way of avoiding the cross. Could not the God of infinite love find for him an avenue of escape? Listen to this prayer: "O my Father, if it be possible, let this cup pass from me: nevertheless not as I will, but as thou wilt." But his second prayer is not a prayer of petition but of acceptance: "O my Father, if this cup may not pass away from me, except I drink it, thy will be done." It is as if Jesus had said: "Inasmuch as this cup cannot pass from me except I drink it, thy will be done." Here once more he accepted the cross as a necessity. Thus his tragic death as seen in prospect was constantly regarded by him as inevitable.

II

Now as Jesus regarded the cross as a necessity when seen in prospect, so he regarded it when seen in retrospect.

When, on the way to Emmaus, he talked with these two friends, the hard ordeal of the Crucifixion had become a fact of history. Its grim anguish was then only a memory. But having passed through death, having experienced the Resurrection, Jesus still regarded the cross not as a needless waste, but as an absolute necessity. Listen to him as he speaks to those who believed that his death had put an end to all their hopes: "O fools, and slow of heart to believe all that the prophets have spoken. Was it not necessary that the Christ should suffer these things?" It was as if he said: "You think that a crucified Christ can do nothing for the world, but the truth is that Christ crucified is the one hope of the world." It was just this conviction on the part of Jesus that his cross was a necessity that enabled him to see in that grim experience not a mere tragedy, but a triumph.

We can glimpse the reason for this when we realize that the degree of bitterness that is born of the tragedies we suffer depends largely upon whether they are needless or necessary. I once read of a father who drove into town with his five-year-old son. To this son he was devoted beyond the ordinary. It so happened that this father met some boon companions and drank more than was his custom. As he drove home he felt especially fit. Almost unconsciously he began to speed. By and by, in an effort to take a curve at high speed, he lost control and plunged down an embankment. He himself was only slightly injured, but his small boy was instantly killed. Of course the loss of his son would have been bitter under any circumstances, but its bitterness was brought to a climax by the fact that the father had to realize that his loss was the result of his own wicked folly.

Here's an exceedingly bitter cry: "O my son Absalom, my son, by son Absalom! would God I had died for thee, O Absalom, my son, my son!" David's heart is broken over the fact that his handsome and gifted boy now lies under a heap of stones in a traitor's grave. But the climax of his sorrow is born of the conviction that the tragedy was needless. Had he not passed his own responsibility onto the shoulders of others, had he only gone in person to look after his son he might have saved him. But this he failed to do. Therefore his loss is doubly bitter because he feels that it might have been avoided.

Now just as tragedy becomes more bitter because of its needlessness, even so it loses somewhat of its bitterness when we know it to be necessary. A few years ago a father was plowing in the field while his two small boys were playing near by. Suddenly he looked up from his work to see a huge dog coming toward the boys. He recognized at once that the dog was mad. Therefore he rushed to meet the oncoming beast, urging his boys to take refuge in a cotton bin. Thus the boys were saved, but the father was bitten from his face to his feet. So completely was he poisoned that medical skill could do nothing for him. But I am told that as the end drew near, in moments when he was free from delirium, he would smile into the face of his wife and say: "Don't you take it too hard. Remember that the boys are safe and that there was no other way." It was the faith of Jesus that through his cross he had accomplished something for us that he could not have accomplished in any other way.

III

If the cross was a necessity why was it so?

Let me begin with this testimony: Christ crucified is my one hope of salvation for time and for eternity. But having said this I make the further confession that I have found no fully satisfactory answer to this question. Of course I know something of what the theologians, past and present, have had to say. They throw light upon it, but I have yet to find an answer that I feel leaves nothing more to be said. It will possibly take much of eternity for the saints to fathom this question. But thank God we do not have to find a fully satisfactory answer to the mystery of the cross in order to reap its benefits.

There are certain answers, I think, that we may renounce altogether. There is, for instance, a superficial reading of the Gospels that has led some to believe that the cross was a necessity in order that the scriptures might be fulfilled. That the cross does fulfill the scriptures few Bible readers will deny. But it was not the scriptures that made the cross a necessity; it was the cross that

140

caused the scriptures thus to be written. I am quite sure that Jesus saw himself as the suffering servant of Jehovah in the fifty-third chapter of Isaiah. But it was not this great chapter that brought about the cross. It was the cross, rather, that gave birth to these words of deathless hope: "He was wounded for our transgressions, he was bruised for our iniquities: the chastisement of our peace was upon him; and with his stripes we are healed."

No more was Jesus crucified because the rulers among his own people and the powers of imperial Rome were too much for him. He died in weakness, but he did not die because of weakness. He makes us sure that life was not wrested from his clinging hands and gripping fingers. Jesus did not lose his life, he gave it. "No man taketh it from me, but I lay it down of myself."

Neither did our Lord die in order to appease the wrath of an angry God. Nothing can be further from the truth than this. It is a slander both against God and against the Son who came to reveal God. We must bear in mind always that the attitude of Jesus toward sinners was the attitude of God the Father. When Jesus prayed: "Father, forgive them; for they know not what they do," that prayer was the will of God. When Jesus was on the cross, God was on the cross. This was the conviction of Paul: "God was in Christ, reconciling the world unto himself." God the Father and God the Son were always at one. They were never more completely so than when Jesus hung by the nails.

Why then, I repeat, was the cross necessary? Of course my answer can be only partial.

141

1. To begin on the human side there came a time when Jesus so clashed with the authorities of his day that he had to go forward to his heroic death or compromise. He knew that it was not necessary for him to live, but that it was necessary that he be true to his own convictions and to the will of God. There was therefore that in his death that makes his suffering akin to that of other heroic souls who have died for conscience's sake. This is not to deny that there is that about the death of Christ that is unshared and unsharable. But there is also that which enables us with Paul to "fill up that which is behind of the afflictions of Christ."

2. Then the cross was a necessity because of who Christ is and who we are. It was impossible for one so sinless and tender of heart as our Lord to live among those so sinful and hard of heart as we are and not suffer the pangs of crucifixion. Further, that great word that he uttered, "Except a corn of wheat fall into the ground and die, it abideth alone" was true for him as for us.

3. But my conviction is that the supreme reason that the cross was a necessity is because God saw in that cross the best possible way of reconciling man to himself. In the light of the cross we see man at his wicked worst. But in this same light we also see man as a creature of infinite worth. At the cross we come face to face with a love that will not let us go. It is a tremendously arresting experience to have any creature love us well enough to be willing to suffer in our behalf. To know that God loves in that fashion is supremely compelling. There is nothing else that at once so wins and breaks our hearts as to be

142

able to say out of our own experiences: "He loved me and gave himself up for me." Herein his own words have been found true: "And I, if I be lifted up from the earth, will draw all men unto me."

IV

Now just as the cross of Jesus is a necessity, so is a proper response on our part a necessity if we are to realize the reconciliation that he died to bring. If you and I give ourselves to him as he gave himself for us, what will it mean to us personally?

1. First, if in response to his self-giving love we dedicate our lives to him, he will accept us and take us into his fellowship. The tragic quarrel between us and God will be ended. Being thus brought into fellowship with him we shall "have peace with God through our Lord Jesus Christ."

2. If we thus yield to God so as to be at peace with him, we shall come to possess inward peace. When we get right with God we get right with ourselves. "There is no peace, saith my God, to the wicked." "The kingdom of God . . . is righteousness, and peace, and joy in the Holy Ghost." There must be rightness with God before there can be peace within. But having thus yielded we can then claim the legacy that Jesus left to his friends: "Peace I leave with you, my peace I give unto you."

3. Finally, having yielded to our self-giving Lord, we not only have peace with God and peace within, but we have peace one with another. It is impossible to look with indifference or scorn or contempt upon any man when we

see in that man a "brother for whom Christ died." The saints of the early church went out to break down all barriers and to bridge all chasms between man and man and race and race. This they did because, having been reconciled themselves, they became ministers of reconciliation. They were ambassadors for Christ. They prayed men in Christ's stead to be reconciled to God. Thus they changed the world. Thus we may help to change it.

XIV

THE IGNORANT PROFESSOR

"Art thou a master of Israel, and knowest not these things?"

JOHN 3:10

❧

IT is amazing how abysmal ignorance can often rub elbows with great learning in the same individual. The fact that one is an authority in a certain field does not make him an authority in another field. Here is a man who was, as another has suggested, at once the equivalent of a college professor, a judge of the supreme court, and a bishop in the church. He was a man of light and learning, yet he was strangely ignorant of the fact that life can be made over. He knew nothing of the new birth. Therefore Jesus asked him very tenderly, I think, and yet with real astonishment: "Art thou a master of Israel, and knowest not these things?"

I

The man of whom Jesus asked this question was named Nicodemus. He represents about the best in the life of his day. He was a man of position and prominence. He be-

145

longed to that cultivated class that gave to the world such scholars as Gamaliel and Paul. He was himself a scholar and a member of the court of the Sanhedrin. He was an honored and religious leader. All in all he was a very fascinating personality.

1. He was a man of open mind. In spite of the fact that he had arrived, so far as position was concerned, he was still intellectually curious. It was his curiosity in part, I think, that caused him to visit Jesus. The Master was just coming into prominence. He had recently cleansed the temple. Strange rumors were blowing about the streets of the city regarding him. Some claimed that he had powers beyond the human. Some declared that he had opened blind eyes and that he had cleansed lepers. Some were even hinting that he might be the long promised Messiah. These rumors excited the curiosity of Nicodemus. Thus curious he was eager for this interview.

Now I have heard curiosity condemned. Of course there is a wrong kind of curiosity. I dare say that not a few have taken their first drink or their first plunge into unclean living out of curiosity. But curiosity in the right direction is good.

> "Twinkle, twinkle little star,
> How I wonder what you are."

Because man wondered he made a telescope and looked at those stars and mapped the heavens. The name of that telescope was Curiosity. It is through the microscope of Curiosity that the scientist searches in his laboratory. It was on the good ship Curiosity that Columbus and Magellan and Admiral Byrd and all the great explorers have sailed. Blessed is the man who is curious to know Jesus!

2. Not only was there curiosity in this visit but intellectual honesty as well. Nicodemus had heard that this new prophet was making strange and stupendous claims, or that at least such claims were being made for him. If these claims were true, this ruler of the Jews, being a religious leader, felt that he ought to know and act accordingly. If they were not true and this exciting man was only an imposter, he ought also to know that and act accordingly. Therefore this curious and honest man turned his feet toward the house where Jesus was stopping.

3. Not only was he curious and intellectually honest, he was also humble. He was willing to learn from anybody who was able to teach him. That is a fine characteristic. In the social scale Jesus and Nicodemus were a long way apart. This ruler of the Jews was an aristocrat; Jesus was a man of the people. Nicodemus had perhaps grown old in leadership, while Jesus was an unknown carpenter. Yet this distinguished man was not too proud to seek this young rabbi out and sit at his feet. It is as if a professor of Harvard University should go down on some mean street in Boston to learn from an obscure person.

4. Then it is evident that this ruler of the Jews, though earnestly religious, was genuinely dissatisfied with himself. Like so many in the church today he could not but realize that his religion had not met his deepest needs. With all his gettings he had not found the best. With all his achievings his heart was still hot and restless and hungry. I think more than all else it was his gnawing

hunger, it was his burning thirst, that sent him down to meet this rabbi from Nazareth.

5. Finally, this professor was possessed of a beautiful type of courage. Commentators differ widely regarding Nicodemus on this point. There are those who argue that he was fearless. They rate his courage at 100 per cent. Then there are others who give him credit for no courage at all. These call attention to the fact that he came to Jesus by night. That his coming by night has significance I think is beyond doubt. This is evidenced by the fact that whenever the author mentions the name of this ruler he reminds us that he came by night.

Why did he come by night? Some who argue that he was fearless affirm that he came by night because he was so desperately in earnest that he could not wait for the coming of the day. Others claim that he came by night because the night was the best time to come. It gave an opportunity for long and uninterrupted conversation. But taking a full view of this ruler I am driven to the conclusion that his timidity was at least a part of the reason for his coming by night. That he was a cautious and timid man I think is evidenced not simply by this scene, but by his next appearance on the stage.

When we next meet him the Pharisees have become thoroughly antagonistic to Jesus. They are out to destory him. They have already sent policemen to arrest him. When these officers return without the prisoner they ask: "Why did you not bring him?" With considerable embarrassment, I imagine, these officers replied: "Never man spoke like this man." At this the Pharisees are thoroughly

148

indignant. "Have any of the authorities or the Pharisees believed in him?" they asked. "But this crowd who do not know the law are accursed."

Then it was that Nicodemus spoke out in the Master's defense: "Does our law judge a man without first giving him a hearing, and learning what he does?" It is not a bold word such as Paul would have spoken. It is not so bold, I dare say, as Nicodemus felt he ought to speak. "Not all Pharisees have rejected him," he might have said, "I have seen him personally, and I am on the way to calling him Lord and Master." But instead of making a bold declaration he only asked a question. This, I think, indicates timidity.

Now the fact that Nicodemus came to Jesus and the further fact that he also spoke out in his defense indicate a high type of courage. For courage at its best is not freedom from fear. A bulldog has that type of courage. Courage at its best is that which leads us to defy our fears. Such was the courage of Nicodemus. He may have come timidly to Jesus. He may have spoken timidly in his defense. But this must not blind us to what really matters and that is that he did come and that he did speak out. The really courageous man is the one who follows the path of duty, even though his knees are shaking with terror.

II

Now suppose we join this cautious scholar as he goes to this interview. He begins the conversation in this fashion: "We know that thou art a teacher come from God." The reply of Jesus to this compliment seems entirely irrelevant.

But the Master is speaking home, not to the words of the professor's lips, but to the longing of his heart. Therefore he replies: "Except a man be born again, he cannot see the kingdom of God." He is saying to this professor: "You are not satisfied. In spite of a life of service to the church you have not found reality. You will never find it until you are born anew."

"How can these things be?" Nicodemus asks in amazement. Jesus is amazed at his amazement. He replies: "Are you a teacher of Israel, and yet you do not understand this?" (R.S.V.) Of course the possibility, the absolute necessity of the new birth is a fundamental truth of our holy religion. That a man can be born again is affirmed not only by the Scriptures, but by modern science as well. The psychologist is now as sure of the new birth as is the evangelist. Of course the psychologist usually calls this experience by a more high-sounding name. But religion and science agree in affirming that a man may be born anew.

To the testimony of the Scriptures and of the psychologists experience adds its voice. The new birth is a fact of experience. All about us are those who are being or have been born anew. There are those, for instance, who are born from beneath. I am thinking now of a lovely young woman I knew years ago. She was an eager worker in my church. To all appearances she was a beautiful Christian. But she became secretary to a man who was a scoundrel. For some years I lost sight of her. When I met her again she had undergone a radical change. Her facial expression was different. Her whole personality had altered. She had become coarse and loud in her talk. She gave me the impression that she had been born anew, born from beneath.

Now just as one may be born from beneath, even so he may be born from above. This new birth is a necessity if one is to see the Kingdom of God. A spiritual birth is just as necessary in order to enter the Kingdom of Heaven as a physical birth in order to enter this world. Therefore no amount of culture, no amount of decency, no amount of devotion, no amount of morality, nothing can take the place of the new birth. It is our greatest privilege. But it is far more than a privilege; it is an absolute necessity.

Having said this it is needful to remind you that we do not all enter this experience in the same fashion. This has been a source of perplexity to many earnest Christians. With some this experience is instantaneous and climactic. As I have dealt with seekers I have seen the light of the glory of God break over their faces as suddenly as a landscape is lighted when a cloud passes from the face of the sun. Many of the great saints have entered into this experience with the suddenness of the lightning's flash. Because this is true there are those who, lacking this climactic experience, fear they have never been converted.

But while many enter into this experience suddenly there are yet more who enter into it gradually. This some are prone to forget. An earnest man said to me some years ago: "I would not give the pop of my finger for any man's religion who cannot tell the day and the hour in which he was converted." How absurd! He might as well have said: "I would not give the pop of my finger for any

151

man's existence who cannot tell the day and the hour in which he was born physically." But it is not the how or the when of the new birth that counts, it is the fact. You might convince me that I am wrong as to the date of my birth, but you could never convince me that I am wrong about the fact of it. If you know the day and the hour in which you were converted, thank God for it. But remember there may be others who are more genuinely conscious of life through Christ than you are, and yet could not fix any birthday. These have blossomed into the knowledge of Christ as flowers bloom at the kiss of spring.

III

What did this interview do for Nicodemus? Does he go away from the presence of this young carpenter singing in his heart with Paul: "Old things have passed away; behold, all things are become new"? Is he conscious of a change within him so great that it can be adequately described only as a passing out of death into life? Has his night given place to glorious day? Has springtime come with life-giving beauty on the wintry hills of his heart? I think we must answer in the negative.

But while he is conscious of no radical change he has been deeply moved. The words of Jesus have thrilled him and have given him new hope. He feels in his soul the fundamental rightness of the man and of what he has said. Therefore when he hears the court, of which he himself is a member, condemn the Master without a hearing, he cannot but speak out in his defense. He does not speak so boldly, I repeat, as he or we should like for him to have

152

spoken. But that timid defense cost him far more than a far bolder speech would have cost a man possessed of a greater natural courage.

Then followed an event so tragic and heartbreaking that it made all the former fears of this ruler seem utterly silly and sinful. Jesus has been done to death in a most ruthless and disgraceful fashion. Nicodemus realizes now that he can never tell him of the loyalty and friendship that through these months have really been in his heart. The help that he could have rendered is now forever impossible. But though he cannot now come "aforetime" as Mary did, he feels that he must do something. Therefore he makes an open confession of loyalty. This he does by assisting at the funeral. He brings a whole hundred-pound weight of myrrh and aloes. That was far too much, but it was his pathetic effort to express his unspoken love and thus atone for the past. I have been called upon to witness many a sorrow, but I have seen few deeper than that of some bereaved and broken heart who vainly seeks to say to the dead what he should have said to the living.

Nicodemus lost much by not coming sooner. But the supremely beautiful fact is that he did come. Thus coming he surely entered into that experience of which Jesus spoke that night when they listened together to the sighing of the night wind. We are sure of this because it was true then as it is true now that "we know, if we follow on to know the Lord." Is this your experience? What Jesus asked in the long ago he is asking today. As a member of the church, as a teacher in the church school, as a minister in the pulpit, do you understand this?

XV

ABSENT WITNESSES

"Woman, where are those thine accusers?
hath no man condemned thee?"

JOHN 8:10

❧

THE scholars are uncertain as to where in the sacred record this story belongs. Some think that it does not belong at all. From certain of the ancient manuscripts it is omitted. However, speaking not as a scholar but merely as a Bible reader, I am sure that it does really belong. Here I feel is a true story. If it is not true it is one from which the truth itself might learn. Not only is this story true, but in my judgment it is factual. It is the record of an event that actually took place. It would have taken a superb genius indeed to have invented a story so true to life. Certainly it is consistent with what we know about the scribes and the Pharisees; it is yet more consistent with what we know about Jesus himself.

It is a sordid story, at least in its beginning. It shows something of the ugliness of human nature. But along with its sordidness it also has a rare beauty. Although some faces in this drama are cruel and hard, there is another that is very strong and tender. If you love a story with a happy ending you would do well to memorize this. If it begins in a black night of storm it ends in the radiant glory of morning. Here a soiled rag of womanhood came to what looked like the end and found it really the "Land of Beginning Again."

I

Look first at the woman who is an unwilling actress in this drama. She is a nameless creature who is an adulteress. Of course there was a partner who shared her sin, but he is not mentioned. He is not even accused. In that day there was a double standard of morals. A man had rights that a woman did not have. Today that is largely changed. Probably the change will eventuate in higher standards for both man and woman. At present woman seems to have dropped nearer to the level of man rather than man climbing to the higher level once occupied by woman.

Not only was this woman guilty, but she had been caught in the act of shame. To be guilty is bad enough, but to be caught is, in the mind of many, worse still. All who knew her knew her guilt. Perhaps she was young. Perhaps she was one who had loved not wisely but too well. Perhaps she was more sinned against than sinning. Or it may be that she was cynical and hard, having walked long in the ways of evil. But whatever the case her sin was known. As her story opens there were eyewitnesses present who could testify against her.

155

Some of these witnesses had laid violent hands on her and had brought her into the presence of Jesus. Having thrust her forward into the limelight they told her story for all to hear. I have an idea that she resisted and resented this bitterly. She may have met Jesus before this humiliating experience. If so she probably dreaded facing him more than she dreaded facing the crowd and these hard men who had dragged her into his presence. Be that as it may, there she is surrounded by a gaping mob, a shamed creature for whom even the religious people of that day had neither care nor hope.

II

The next group of actors in this drama is made up of the witnesses for the prosecution. They are the men who have dragged the woman into the presence of Jesus. They are the scribes and the Pharisees. As a rule these two classes do not show up well on the pages of the New Testament. Yet because of this we are not to conclude that there was nothing good about them. There was much to be said in their favor. They were the upholders of the law. They were pillars in church and state. It was a part of their business to oppose such evil conduct as that of which this woman was guilty.

Along with much that was good in these scribes and Pharisees there was also much that was evil. In the first place, in this particular instance their motives were bad. They claimed to be acting out of zeal for the law; they wanted a clean individual and social life. But their real motive was their desire to involve Jesus in difficulty.

156

They were eager to discredit this young teacher whose popularity was causing them no end of trouble. In claiming to be concerned about the woman, while they were really bent only on embarrassing the Master, they were playing the hypocrite.

Not only were they hypocritical, but they were cold as icicles and hard as nails. In perpetrating this plot against Jesus they involved this woman in a very real and painful embarrassment. Yet they were totally indifferent to the woman herself. She was to them only "Exhibit A." They had involved her in this humiliating situation not because they were indignant at her sin; no more did they involve her because they were seeking by her punishment to build a cleaner community; least of all were they seeking by thus bringing her to Jesus to do her any real good. To her, I repeat, they were entirely indifferent. To them she was a creature beyond hope or help. Therefore her pain and shame in being thus exposed meant to them just nothing at all.

Now while they had not sinned as their victim had sinned they were still sinners. Theirs was the sin of disposition; hers was that of the flesh. These two kinds of sinners are always with us. We are accustomed to condemn those who sin after the flesh far more severely than those who sin by their indifference and coldness of heart. But this was not the case with Jesus. He seems to have hated and feared most the sins of the disposition. To his mind the decent and respectable elder son who had remained at home was far more hopeless than the prodigal who in penitence had come back after wasting his sub-

stance with riotous living. Jesus therefore had more hope
for this woman than for her decent and respectable tormentors.

III

But the real center of the story is Jesus. When these
men fling their victim at the feet of the Master they put to
him a question: "The law of Moses," they declare, "com-
mands that such creatures shall be stoned, but what do
you say?" It is evident that these scribes and Pharisees
know something about Jesus. They know enough to make
them quite certain of the position he will take with regard
to this woman. They are sure that he will be on the side
of mercy. It is this conviction that accounts for their
coming. They realized that if Jesus should agree with the
law and say: "Yes, stone her by all means," then, by their
scheme they would not embarrass him, but only add to his
reputation. But they are certain that, in spite of what the
law says, Jesus will not order her to be stoned.

In taking this position they were not mistaken. When
they put their question, "Stone her or not stone her?" the
Master gives no immediate answer. Instead he stoops
down and writes on the ground. Why he does this we are
not told. In my opinion he does it for two reasons. First,
he is ashamed of these religious leaders. They are here
as the representatives of God. Yet how terribly and trag-
ically do they misrepresent him! Second, he is seeking to
spare this woman. He sees how bitterly ashamed she is.
Therefore he refuses to add to her embarrassment by
looking at her. Those who enjoy another's shame are not

158

like Jesus. He suffered in the shame of others, even that of this fallen woman.

When these scribes and Pharisees see Jesus thus writing on the ground and refusing to answer they are sure that they have gained their point. Therefore they begin to press him more urgently. "Shall we stone her or not stone her?" It is a yes or no question, as you can see. They are shrewd enough to know that if they can induce him to say either "Yes" or "No," they will have achieved their purpose. But he refuses to fall into their trap.

Nowhere does Jesus show his genius more convincingly than in the way in which he answered questions. Once his disciples asked: "Are there few that be saved?" They desired his yes or no, but Jesus did not so answer. He rather said: "Strive to enter in at the straight gate." He meant: "How many are saved or how few is not your business. Your business is to meet the conditions of salvation yourselves." Again they asked, "Is it lawful to give tribute to Caesar, or not?" Instead of answering "Yes" or "No" he requested a penny. When they handed him one he asked whose image was upon it. "Caesar's," they answered. "Right," he seemed to say, "therefore render to Caesar the things that are Caesar's, and to God the things that are God's."

Notice how Jesus answers the question of these scribes and Pharisees. He certainly is opposed to the stoning of this woman, yet he does not say so in so many words. Jesus never antagonized except when it was necessary. Had he forbidden them to stone her he would have alienated her tormentors, while leaving them utterly unconvinced of the rightness of his position. Bear in mind that he is just as eager to save these evil men as he is to save the woman.

Sometimes we congratulate ourselves for speaking our minds. That is all to the good if we have the right stuff in our minds and if we are convinced that our speaking will prove helpful. But there are times when speaking our minds does more harm than good.

With what sanity and tact Jesus meets this issue! "Stone her," he seems to say, "by all means, provided you yourselves are guiltless. Let him that is without sin cast the first stone. But of course if you are sinful you do not dare to throw a single stone." How utterly sane! What could be more absurd than for one sinner to stone another sinner? Of course we differ in the kinds of sin of which we are guilty and we differ in the degree of guilt, but all of us in some fashion are sinners. Therefore throwing stones either with our hands or with our tongues is never in order. It is neither sane nor Christian.

Then what? Convinced of the essential rightness of the position of Jesus, these witnesses against the accused slipped away one by one. Who is declaring now that the law of Moses ought to be enforced? Not the Master, but these scribes and Pharisees. By his wise answer Jesus not only cuts the ground from under them so far as bringing charges against himself is concerned, but he even brings them over to his side. By their own actions they are declaring that this unfortunate creature ought not to be stoned, at least not by themselves.

When the scribes and Pharisees are gone comes the big

moment for which the Master had waited. He now stands erect and looks at the woman for the first time. Then he asks: "Woman, where are those, thine accusers? hath no man condemned thee?" I can hear her answer with a sob in her throat: "No man, Lord." With none to testify against her she has hope of winning her case.

IV

Why does Jesus ask about these absent witnesses? He is certainly not seeking information. He is rather seeking to bring to fruition the faith that has already been born in the heart of this woman. What has been going on in her mind during this trying ordeal? I think that she has come to realize that the man into whose presence she has been dragged so unwillingly, whose frown she has so greatly feared, is really on her side—that he is not her enemy but her friend. Here perhaps is what she is saying to herself: "These hard men have let me go. They have forgiven me, thanks to the fact that Jesus has taken my part. Since they have forgiven in their way, perhaps he will forgive in his far fuller way." And that is just what he does. Here are his own words: "Neither do I condemn thee: go, and sin no more."

There are those who feel that the woman got off too easily, that Jesus is here treating sin as a rather light matter. It reminds one of Maeterlinck's picture of God as lolling at his ease and watching the follies and even the crimes of men as one might watch the playful antics of puppies. But Jesus never made light of sin. Why then did the Master let her off so easily? Because there was no

161

other way. Forgiveness is a gift. None of us, even the best, can ever earn it. What could this woman do toward turning back the leaves of the sordid book of her past and blotting out the ugly writing? Nothing at all.

> "The Moving Finger writes; and, having writ,
> Moves on: nor all your Piety nor Wit
> Shall lure it back to cancel half a line,
> Nor all your Tears wash out a Word of it."

What then are we to do about our sin? We are to do what this woman did. We are to accept the forgiveness of God and then turn our back upon that sin and forget it. When God forgives he forgets. This is his promise: "I will forgive their iniquity, and I will remember their sin no more." What God forgets you and I have a right to forget. This is in part what Paul meant when he said: "Forgetting those things which are behind, and reaching forth unto those things which are before, I press toward the mark for the prize."

Here then was a poor creature who had been dragged into the presence of Jesus, filled with shame and terror. She felt that she had reached the end of everything. There was not even a horizon in her life where she might hope for a dawn. But thanks to the forgiving love of Christ she found that it was not the closing in of night, but the dawning of a new day. Thus with boundless joy she planted her feet upon the borders of the "Land of Beginning Again." So may we if we dare to turn from the past, and in the fellowship of our Lord make a new start.

XVI

THE LUSTERLESS JEWEL

"Know ye what I have done to you?"

JOHN 13:12

❧

WHAT had he done?
The story takes us back across the far spaces of the years to an upper room in the city of Jerusalem. Here Jesus has come with his disciples for the last Passover that they will ever celebrate together. There is about this scene the solemnity that goes naturally with dear last things. But there is far more. Here Jesus dares to displace the paschal lamb and to put himself in its place. This he does as he breaks the bread and puts a piece in the hand of each of his disciples saying in effect: "This is my body, my very self, my all, given for you." Thus this is a sacred and solemn meal, one that they share under the very shadow of the cross.

Since this is the case it is shocking to realize the spirit in which these disciples have come to this great hour. They have not come in humility; they have come rather with glowing cheeks and burning eyes. They have come hissing hot words at each other. They have come arguing over who is to be the greatest, who is to be chairman of the committee, who is to head the delegation. Each one is pridefully contending for what he conceives to be his own rights.

Now this was probably a secret meeting, and there were no servants present to wash the feet of the guests. James and John might have volunteered for this menial task. Only recently, when they had sought first places for themselves, Jesus had told them that the one way to be first was to be servant of all. But they seem to have forgotten this. Therefore I would have been afraid to have suggested that they perform this task lest by so doing I should come to a better understanding of why the Master called them "sons of thunder." No more would I have dared make this suggestion to Simon, the natural leader of the group. Every man among them was too busy asserting his own rights, standing upon his dignity. Then it was that Jesus took the lowly task upon himself.

This he did not because he liked being a martyr. Jesus humbled himself here, as he humbled himself later by going to the cross, because there was no other way to put through a task that needed to be done. It is said that President Lincoln was walking one day with a friend along a path that was so narrow that the two had to walk single file. By and by they met another man. When this man kept the path Lincoln had to stand aside. The friend was indignant. "Mr. President," he said, "you should not have done that. You ought to have made him stand aside." "But," said the president, "had I not stood aside there

164

would have been a collision." Even so, Jesus saw that if he did not take this task upon himself it would simply be left undone.

"Know ye what I have done to you?" Jesus asks after he has resumed his place. What is the answer? He has rendered them a service that none other was big enough to render. By so doing he has taught them a lesson in humility. I am sorry I cannot find a more glamourous name for this fine jewel. Humility has such little glitter for most of us that it fails to thrill us. We tend to regard it as a pious church coin, worth perhaps a hundred cents in the dollar at prayer meeting, but far below par everywhere else. For this reason if one were to call us humble we would hardly know whether to feel complimented or insulted. If this virtue is a rare jewel it is one that for our eyes has largely lost its luster.

I

What do we mean by humility?

To begin negatively it is something that these disciples did not possess. Humility is certainly not a clamoring for first place. No more is it a prideful refusal to do a task just because it is menial. It is not a swaggering demand for position. It is not that spirit that often leads men to say: "If I can't be chairman of the committee I won't serve."

If humility is not self-glorification, no more is it self-contempt. There are those who think they are humble just because they say mean things about themselves. This is not humility. It is only an ugly caricature of humility. No man is in a better frame of mind to make a failure of life than the man who has no self-respect.

Look at the attitude of our Lord when he performed this task: "Jesus, knowing that the Father had given all things into his hands, and that he was come from God, and went to God; he riseth from supper, and laid aside his garments; and took a towel, and girded himself." Does that sound like self-contempt? At the very moment when he was most keenly conscious of his divine origin and of his divine destiny he stooped to do this slave's task. But he did not stoop in the spirit of a slave. Never was one girded with a higher self-respect. What then is humility?

1. Humility is the natural and inevitable result of facing the facts about ourselves. It has been suggested that while humility is based upon the truth, pride is founded on a lie. What are the facts about ourselves?

First, we are all the children of God. We are made in the divine image. Thus we are grand creatures. Listen how the psalmist puts it: "What is man, that thou art mindful of him? . . . Thou hast made him a little lower than the angels." Moffatt translates it "little less than divine." Not only are we grand creatures, made in the image of God, but we have been redeemed by the precious blood of Christ. Thus redeemed, we are to reproduce Christ. We are to say with Paul: "For to me to live is Christ."

But there is a second fact that we must face and that is that we have not lived up to our privileges. Though made for Christlikeness we have failed to realize our possibilities. In spite of the fact that it is the purpose of God that the beauty of the Lord should rest upon us as the sunshine rests upon the hills, we are far less winsome than we have any right to be. Paul declares that all of us have "come short." Most of us are not disposed to deny that. However much we may have attained we are yet only poor fractions of what we might be.

There is a story of a great artist who went one morning to a picture gallery where his own pictures were on display. He went early to avoid the crowd. But as he was going away a friend saw him. The artist sought to avoid this friend, but in vain. The friend understood the reason when he saw the artist's face wet with tears.

"What is the matter?" he asked.

"I have been looking at my own pictures," came the answer. "Those that I painted in my youth give a promise that I have failed to realize in my mature years. It is heartbreaking to face the fact that I have not become the artist that I might have become."

When we thus see ourselves in the light of what we might be, humility is a natural result.

2. Humility is childlikeness. First, a child is teachable. A child is willing to learn from anybody. A child is willing to lean upon a higher power. He is not self-sufficient. He realizes his weakness. I saw a little fellow run ahead of his mother on the street the other day, but when he came to a crossing he was not ashamed to reach his hand up to the hand of his mother. A child is willing to lean on a higher power.

Second, to be childlike is to be democratic. A child is free from snobbery. No normal child ever refuses to play with another child because that child is inferior in wealth or in social position. He does not stand aloof because he is of a different race or color. He is as much at home with the son of a pauper as the son of a king. Humility is child-likeness.

3. Humility is Christlikeness. Humility is the one virtue in himself to which our Lord calls our attention. "Learn of me; for I am meek and lowly in heart." So humble was he that he did this menial task of foot washing when nobody else would do it. So humble was he that "though he was divine by nature, he did not set store upon equality with God, but emptied himself by taking the nature of a servant; born in human guise and appearing in human form, he humbly stooped in his obedience even to die, and to die even upon the cross." (Moffatt.) To be humble is to be Christlike. It is to forget self in an effort to serve others.

II

Why is this virtue so priceless?

1. It is priceless because it is the very door into the kingdom of heaven. "Blessed are the poor in spirit: for theirs is the kingdom of heaven." The humble enter the Kingdom because they are capable of entering it, and no others are. Listen to this story: "Two men went up into the temple to pray; the one a Pharisee, and the other a publican. The Pharisee stood and prayed thus with himself, God, I thank thee, that I am not as other men are, extortioners, unjust, adulterers. . . . The publican, standing afar off, would not lift up so much as his eyes unto

heaven, but smote upon his breast, saying, God be merciful to me a sinner. I tell you, this man went down to his house justified rather than the other."

Why did the publican win while the Pharisee failed? It was certainly not because of any superiority on the part of this publican. The Pharisee was a far better man. He was upright and decent. He was a tither. But for him and men of his type there would have been no temple to which the publican could turn in his black hour. That which defeated him, in spite of much that was good, was his lack of humility. He asked for nothing because he needed nothing. Having already arrived he could not go any higher. This publican, on the other hand, entered the Kingdom in spite of his great sin because he was poor in spirit. It is only the humble who can enter and remain in the Kingdom. In the face of all others the door is shut.

There is nothing surprising about this. Humility conditions our entrance into all worth-while kingdoms. How do we enter the kingdom of knowledge? Only by the door of humility. I used to teach school. I am sure teachers will agree with me that the most difficult pupil is not the one who is a bit dull. The most difficult is the one who already knows, the one who was born educated. How did Huxley learn science? He tells us that he sat down before the facts as a little child.

Then humility is of value not only in the church and in the classroom, but in the world of business. I was reading recently of a man of ability who worked up from the ranks. He came to own a small railroad. He bought that road when it was bankrupt and made it a going concern. But he was so arrogant and overbearing that he could not get on with his employees. For this reason he sleeps today in an untimely grave. The man who gets on best is the man who is willing to learn, not only from his employer, but from his humblest employee as well.

Humility is as essential in making and keeping friends. If you are an egotist, if you play superior to those with whom you associate, you need not expect to have friends. This virtue is also necessary in the family circle. If either husband or wife is always right while the other is always wrong, if one has to sit at the feet of the other, there is tragedy present and greater tragedy ahead. Humility therefore is essential not only in prayer meeting but everywhere else. It is the door into all worth-while kingdoms and it is an essential for abiding in those kingdoms.

2. Humility is essential to our happiness. Sometimes we are proud of our pride. We look askance at the word of Jesus, "Blessed are the poor in spirit." But even if you question the happiness of those who are humble. you cannot question the wretchedness of those who are proud. If you are forever standing on your dignity, if you are forever demanding recognition and appreciation, if you are bent on getting credit for everything you do, then you are headed for a stormy voyage. This is the case because however much honor and applause may come your way there will always be something to wound your pride.

3. Finally, humility is essential to our usefulness. This is true for a variety of reasons.

First, it is the humble who are most willing to serve.

Of course the proud will serve if the applause is sufficiently loud. They will serve if they gain proper recognition. They will serve if the task is not beneath them. But the humble will serve unconditionally. All they ask is for a task that needs to be done.

Second, the humble are most useful because their right attitude makes their service acceptable. We seldom help anybody by reaching down to him from superior heights. I had a friend in college who had deep wounds upon his soul because of an unhappy childhood. He had grown up in the midst of domestic conflict and heartache. While outwardly sunny, he told me in a hour of confidence that for years he had never gone to bed at night that he did not wish that he might not wake in the morning. With this battered soul I went to hear a brilliant minister preach. His sermon was eloquent but as we came away my friend declared that the minister reminded him of one standing at a safe distance on the shore and shouting to another who was drowning: "You fool, you had no business falling in." There could be no sharper criticism than that.

Finally, the humble are most helpful because of their right attitude toward God. The man who sets out on a mission of service, trusting only in his own sufficiency, must needs go alone. But the humble man goes in the strength of Almighty God. By his humility he enables our Lord to make good his promise: "Lo, I am with you alway even unto the end of the world."

XVII

CHANGING HEARSAY INTO EXPERIENCE

"Sayest thou this thing of thyself, or did others tell it thee of me?"

JOHN 18:34

ご~の

THIS is a dramatic scene. Pilate is standing face to face with a prisoner who is none other than Jesus Christ. The moment therefore is one big with possibilities. Strange and disquieting rumors have been blowing about the streets of Jerusalem concerning this man. One report has it that some of his most enthusiastic followers, with more rashness than reason, had escorted him into the city with cries of "Hosanna to the son of David: blessed is he that cometh in the name of the Lord." Pilate, knowing the tempestuous temperament of the people under his authority, has found these rumors a bit disquieting. Yet he cannot feel that Rome has much to fear from a man just out of a carpenter shop, with only a handful of peasants at his back.

But now that Pilate stands face to face with Jesus he

finds him strangely disturbing. If this man is a pretender he is certainly not like any other that Pilate has met before. In spite of himself this Roman governor is impressed. Therefore with mingled awe and amazement he asks Jesus this question: "Art thou the King of the Jews?" In reply Jesus asks the governor this daring and searching question: "Sayest thou this thing of thyself, or did others tell it thee of me?" It is as if he says: "Pilate, are you speaking from hearsay or out of your own experience? Am I your king?"

That, I repeat, is a daring question. It is evident that Jesus had hope for Pilate. When our Lord was questioned by Herod he answered never a word. Jesus knew that Herod had stopped his ears to the truth so long that he had lost his capacity to hear, that he had shut his eyes to the light so long that he had gone blind. But the Master saw fine possibilities in Pilate. He believed that this Roman governor was yet capable of a high choice. Therefore he held open the door of his Kingdom to him with this question: "Sayest thou this thing of thyself, or did others tell it thee of me?" Thus Jesus invited Pilate to change hearsay into experience. Pilate was impressed, but he was not impressed enough to make the change.

Now there is a sense in which this story is entirely unique. Yet there is also that in it that comes very near to everyone. We, as avowed followers of this Christ, have united with his church, have acknowledged his kingship. But is that kingship a reality? In other words, is your religion a matter of hearsay or of experience? If it is only hearsay then you have missed the highest and the best.

This is not to say that hearsay is of no value. It is of vast value. But in the realm of religion it is not enough.

I

What is the good of hearsay?

We are indebted to hearsay for almost all the small knowledge we possess. How much, for instance, do you know about history? Very little at first hand. I am told that there was once a man named Julius Caesar who waged a campaign in Gaul. I am told further that this same Julius Caesar wrote commentaries about his campaign. These commentaries have been the plague of many a schoolboy. But whether Julius Caesar really wrote them or not is impossible for me to say. The one thing about them of which I can be sure is that somebody wrote them and that they gave me no end of trouble. I do not even know who discovered America except from hearsay. This is the case because whoever made the discovery beat me to it. I must depend on hearsay for this as for almost every other fact in history.

In like manner I take the little I know about astronomy from hearsay. I am told that the sun is 92,900,000 miles from the earth. I am told also that this sun has a temperature at its surface of about 12,000 degrees Fahrenheit. But I have never tested the truth of either of these statements. I never intend to. I am quite sure that even if the astronomers are a few feet off in their measurement one way or the other, life will go on for me practically the same. I am equally certain that if in estimating the temperature of the sun they have made a mistake of one or two degrees, it will not greatly upset the noiseless tenor of my way. In matters of astronomy I take the word of the astronomers.

We have a saying that runs like this: "I am willing to take your word for that." So I am in a great many matters. For instance, I am told that if I hold my hand on a red-hot stove it will not only be very painful, but the hand will receive permanent injury. I will take your word for that. I do not intend to try it. There is a drink that, according to scientists, seems to stimulate while it really depresses. When a motorist takes it he thinks he is more fit to cope with an emergency, while in reality he becomes less fit because all his reactions have been slowed down. There are those who become victims to this drink. Such people it masters and enslaves, rots them down both in body and soul. But all this I take on hearsay. I never intend to put this drink to the test.

Naturally there are those who do not agree with me. They must find out for themselves. If a cocktail is offered in a social circle they take it. Sometimes they begin the custom from curiosity. Sometimes they begin because they feel that it would be a discourtesy to refuse. A young woman complained of how terribly embarrassing it is to have to make such refusals. But it seems to me that all the embarrassment should be on the other side. At least I believe that I have just as much right to my convictions as the other man has to his lack of convictions. Nor do I think it a matter of shame when I refuse to take a needless risk. If my hostess were to say to me: "Here is a sandwich; it is spread with a high-grade poison," I should not be tempted in the least to do other than take her word for it.

Even in matters of religion hearsay is priceless. It is such hearsay that makes this book we call the Bible the most precious in all the world. Listen to this: "I sought the Lord, and he heard me, and delivered me from all my fears." Just what fears were yapping at the heels of this frightened psalmist he does not see fit to tell us. He does tell us, however, that as he called on God the whole wolf pack took flight. That is only hearsay, but it is hearsay that warms my heart and gives me hope. We must all be unspeakably grateful for the hearsay that comes to us out of the Scriptures.

Priceless also is the testimony of the saints throughout the centuries. We all owe to them an unpayable debt. How greatly we are enriched by the testimonies of those whom we have known personally! I can never be sufficiently thankful for the God-possessed men and women whom I have known along the way. I am being constantly strengthened, gladdened, and encouraged by the faith of others. Certainly hearsay in the realm of religion is of vast importance. Rightly used it will lead to the supreme enrichment. Yet hearsay is not enough. To achieve its purpose it must be changed into experience.

II

Why is this the case?

1. This is the case, in the first place, because it is only experience that can satisfy the human soul. It is well to know about God. Theology is the queen of all sciences.

Yet no knowledge about God can take the place of knowing God himself. I may be an expert on bread. I may know all about its food value and how to prepare it, but not even the most perfect knowledge of bread can satisfy my hunger. However much I may know about water, my tongue will become swollen, my lips parched, my body tortured to the point of death unless I experience water by actually drinking it. It is fine to know about flowers. Botany is a lovely study. But no knowledge of botany can take the place of the perfume of the honeysuckle, nor the red of the rose. Even so, no knowledge about God can take the place of knowing God through Christ.

When therefore the psalmist sings: "As the hart panteth after the water brooks, so panteth my soul after thee, O God," he is voicing a universal longing. When Job wails: "Oh that I knew where I might find him!" he is uttering a cry that has sobbed its way through the centuries. When Philip prays: "Lord, shew us the Father," he is praying a prayer that is as old as man. It has been offered in some fashion by men of every age and of every kindred, tribe, and tongue.

What is the matter with our tired and restless world? If Isaiah were to appear on our streets today would he not search us with his question of long ago: "Wherefore do ye spend money for that which is not bread? and your labour for that which satisfieth not?" Our world is fretful and hungry for something or someone that it has not found. This is true even of many people in our churches. Some of you have not found in religion what you once hoped to find. You are absolutely certain that the Lord is

177

a shepherd, but there is no song in your heart because you have not yet learned to sing "The Lord is my shepherd." You are certain that God loves all men, but you have not yet come to say out of your own experience that he "loved me, and gave himself for me." Hearsay is good, but unless we translate it into experience we never come to that spiritual certainty that alone can satisfy.

2. In the second place it is only those who change hearsay into experience who have an adequate passion for the sharing of their experience with others. To know any worth-while fact is to be possessed by an eagerness to share our knowledge. When Galileo was being tortured for saying that the earth moves around the sun he recanted. But as soon as the agony of his torture was eased he reaffirmed his original conviction. Being sure, he had to share.

If such eagerness to share the truth is characteristic of the scientist, it is even more so of one who has found reality in religion. Do you remember that leper of whom Mark tells? Life had dealt very harshly with him. It had dealt so harshly that though he still believed in power he no longer believed in love. So he came to the Master with this imperfect prayer: "If thou wilt, thou canst make me clean." Jesus responded to his imperfect faith and healed him. Having healed him the Master gave him this warning: "See thou say nothing to any man." So what? The healed man simply could not keep his secret. I have an idea that he fairly shouted to the first man he met: "Look at me! A little while ago I was a leper; now my flesh is like that of a little child. I am cured." So did he blaze his

178

story abroad that the Master could no longer openly enter the city.

It was this certainty that gave voice to the great prophets of the Old Testament. Some of them spoke with intense reluctance. Take Jeremiah, for instance. So little did his preaching seem to accomplish, except to make the preacher hated, that more than once he made up his mind to quit. "What is the use?" he said to himself. "Those to whom I preach do not repent; they only hate and persecute me. I will never preach again." But as often as he made that resolution he had to break it. This he did because the Word of God was as a fire shut up in his bones. The burning convictions of his heart made silence impossible.

This same passion for telling their story belongs emphatically to those whom we meet on the pages of the New Testament. Here are two of them before the same court that a few weeks ago had sentenced their Master to death. The court decides to give these two offenders a light sentence. They simply command them not to speak at all, nor teach in the name of Jesus. But Peter and John answer: "We cannot but speak the things which we have seen and heard." They are under the urge of a mighty assurance. They are in the grip of a compelling certainty. It is easy to keep silent about a religion of hearsay, but you can no more silence a religion of experience than you can dam up Niagara.

3. Not only do we need to change hearsay into experience to satisfy the longing of our own hearts and to give us an adequate passion for sharing our experiences, but we need to do this in order to have power for wit-

nessing. There is something compelling about a man who has made himself master of a subject, whatever that subject is. How gripping is the message of the man who brings fresh and authentic tidings of God! When the crowd turned away from hearing Jesus they said with awe: "He taught them as one having authority, and not as the scribes." What was wrong with the scribes? Their religion was largely a matter of hearsay. But Jesus could say always what he said to Nicodemus: "We speak that we do know, and testify that we have seen."

It was this same note of authority that enabled the early saints to turn the world upside down. Who would ever have chosen a Samaritan woman of such a soiled past for an evangelist? Yet when she left her water vessel and hurried into the village, she was so sure of Jesus that we read: "Many . . . believed on him for the saying of the woman." Thomas loved Jesus with all his big heart. But he would have been worth little as a witness had he not come to say to the risen Christ: "My Lord and my God." The power of Paul to convince men of his day and of all days was born not so much of his great ability as of his great certainty. The fact that he could say: "I know whom I have believed," made him a man of power. This same certainty is needed by us. We are not going to make any great dent on our hard world by the proclamation of a gospel that is only hearsay.

III

Is this certainty possible for us? If so, how can we find it?

It is my conviction that this certainty is possible for every one of us. This is not to say that all men have an equal capacity to realize God. There are some who see with clearer vision than others. But all men can realize him in some fashion. "If any man is willing to do his will, he shall know." This promise is not for certain elect souls who have a special aptitude for religion. It is for any man, for every man who is willing to do his will.

Not only does this word tell us that religious certainty is for everybody, but it also indicates the conditions upon which we may possess such certainty. In order to be sure of God it is not necessary to be perfect, it is only necessary to be willing wholeheartedly to do the will of God. If we are to realize God we must make a complete surrender to him. We must be willing to put ourselves and all we have into his hands. To all such God gives himself. "We are his witnesses of these things; and so is also the Holy Ghost, whom God hath given to them that obey him."

Sometimes this awareness of God comes instantly. Those who have been accustomed to dealing with seeking souls personally can testify that they have seen men pass instantly into a knowledge of God. But such instantaneous awareness does not always come. There are those who, having surrendered, become aware of God gradually. The light that breaks on them is more like the slow dawning day. But if any man surrenders, and persists in that surrender, he will come to certainty. He will realize the truth of those words from Hosea: "Then shall we know, if we follow on to know the Lord." Every one of us can thus change hearsay into experience.